The
Christian Meaning
of Human Sexuality

By Paul M. Quay, S.J., Ph.D.

IGNATIUS PRESS   SAN FRANCISCO

Previous English edition: 1985
Credo House Books
Evanston, Illinois

Imprimi potest: J. Leo Klein, S.J., Provincial
Chicago Province

Imprimatur: + Joseph T. O'Keefe, D.D.
Vicar-General
Archdiocese of New York

Nihil Obstat: William B. Smith, S.T.D.
Censor Librorum

Cover by Riz Boncan Marsella

ISBN 0−89870−212−7
Library of Congress catalogue number 88−81092
Printed in the United States of America

CONTENTS

Preface

This little book attempts to sketch, without learned apparatus, the understanding of human sexuality that divine revelation offers us.

It is intended primarily for Christian adults who wish not only to know what kinds of sexual behavior are right or wrong but to gain true insight into *why* such behavior is right or wrong for those who seek to love and live in Christ. For, sexual morality is part of the mystery of our life in Christ and makes full sense only when seen as such.

The approach taken here bypasses, without denying, the usual ethical and natural-law types of arguments. Since understanding of the Christian mystery, so far as we are given access to it, is offered us through the Scriptures and the living Tradition of the Church, my effort has been to show what sexuality means for the Christian in terms of the Scriptures and a most important part of the Tradition, the teaching of the Fathers of the early Church.

The Fathers were at one in teaching, in an endless variety of ways, that sexual activity by Christians is meant to mirror the relations between each of the divine Persons and the Church, and that these relations constitute the most basic meaning of any right sexual activity.

Theoretical justification for this approach can be found in other things I have written, listed in the References on page 113. But all of that is left aside here, where we wish simply to set forth the deep reasons given us by God in His revelation for the moral teachings of His Church on sex.

Preface

Finally, I wish to thank the host of people who, over the years, have selflessly supported and urged forward the writing and publication of this book. Many have offered me their own ideas, experience, and suggestions, have commented on or zealously promoted what was written already, have given financial support, have heartened me by their interest and gracious encouragement, have been praying for the Lord's help and blessing. It is my fault alone that this mountain of goodness has brought forth such a small mouse of a book. Please accept my gratitude and be assured of my continuing prayers.

Paul M. Quay, S.J.
Loyola University of Chicago
Feast of St. John Bosco, 1984

1

Christ: the Image and Likeness of God

THE UNIQUENESS OF CHRISTIAN SEXUAL BEHAVIOR AND ITS SOCIAL IMPORT

From the time of our Lord Himself, Christians' attitudes and behavior in sexual matters have perplexed the people around them. The apostles were baffled when our Lord, speaking of divorce-and-remarriage, declared it to be adultery. If so, they thought, it would be better for a man not to marry. His whole audience was probably baffled when He said, "You have heard that it was said, 'You shall not commit adultery.' But I say to you that everyone who looks at a woman lustfully has already committed adultery with her in his heart." This is certainly tightening up the Law beyond all expectation. The leaders of His people were undoubtedly puzzled when He said, "For your hardness of heart, Moses allowed you to divorce your wives, but from the beginning it was not so." By these words and His immediate rejection of remarriage, He set up man's state in Eden before the fall as a norm for our behavior. This teaching was shocking even to a people that Scripture itself says were well prepared for His coming.

Consequently, when this teaching moved out through the apostles and the early Christians into the pagan world, it was misunderstood, fought, and often very bitterly resented. The result, frequently, was martyrdom for those who insisted upon preserving their virginity or their chastity. So much was this the case that virginity or chastity was regarded by the pagans as a touchstone to identify Christians. Those who would not take part in the unchaste actions of their fellows or who preferred virginity to marriage were marked immediately as Christians and sent to the lions.

On the other hand, the martyrs never regarded chastity as that for which they died. Chastity, simply in itself, was a small thing in their eyes. It was their love for Christ, who wanted them to be chaste, that gave them their determination to be chaste. Their chastity was part of their witness to the Lord. Thus, when the bloody martyrdoms were over, many Christians withdrew to the desert to be witnesses again to Christ and to His love for us; and again, virginity or chaste celibacy was a part of that witness. We ourselves should not be wholly amazed if, some day, chastity might cost us our lives, even as it cost the early Christians theirs or, in our own time, St. Maria Goretti hers.

From the earliest days till now, the Church has been firm on these matters. There has been many a difficulty within the Church, many a dispute and contention, and many a loss of members because of her firmness on points of sexual morality that the world, by and large, saw as unimportant, as matters of personal preference. So it is today also. The Church continues to insist that the entire area of sexual attitudes and behavior is of utmost importance.

It is most unlikely, then, that we can ever fit in with

the world around us in matters of sex, if we really know what it is to be Christian—though too often we may have reason to be ashamed that we are not living as chastely as some pagans. If, then, we find that we are not at odds with the world, by and large, in our sexual behavior, we can be sure we are not living as good Christians. For Christ has given us both understanding and power concerning chastity that the world not only does not accept, but frequently cannot accept.

Though human sexuality, like that of brute animals, exists for the sake of procreation and the bondings biologically necessary for raising the young, it has social aspects far wider than anything found among beasts.

Perceptive Catholics today, who once might have thought of chastity as important only for individuals in their efforts to keep the commandments and practice virtue, have become keenly aware that recent weakenings of sexual restraint have given rise to grave social problems.

The controversy stirred up in response to *Humanae Vitae*, for example, has shown that private sexual problems can have major public effects not only on the Church but on civil society and the whole culture.

The nature of the Church itself was called into question as soon as sex was thought to be a private matter, to be dealt with solely by the consciences of individual couples. For, if sex is merely private, then, as we shall see, the relations between God and His Church are merely private. Whence the Church, as anything more than a private gathering of like-minded individuals, would cease to exist.

As to civil society, had Catholics not been publicly divided on *Humanae Vitae* by the efforts of dissenting clergy and religious, one may well wonder whether the Supreme Court would have decided *Roe* v. *Wade* in favor of unrestricted abortion. But when Christians doubt, vacillate, and lack conviction as to what sex means or how to find that meaning in practice, those who have no doubts move in and make the decisions for society.

It seems no accident that our culture, which has long seen religion as essentially a private matter, whatever help it may gain from community support, should have come to its present notions of marriage also as essentially a private matter. Hence have come the shattering of families through divorce-with-remarriage, the abortions (legally justified by the Supreme Court, recall, on the grounds of "privacy"), the killings of "defective" infants and the incurably ill (increasingly tolerated on the same grounds of "privacy"), all of which result from making sexual action a private matter, outside the scope of the law to regulate. As a result, the "right to privacy" concedes to individuals powers over the lives of others that no state could ever legitimately exercise itself. "Privacy" has become the current euphemism for absolute and murderous individualism.

The great irony is that, as with other areas of individualism, government has now taken over from the jealous individualist, without his protest, what he would not allow to his family, friends, or the Church. Government ratification and enforcement of total privacy in sexual behavior has now made sex a public affair.

The federal government formerly had no function with regard to sexual matters; and even state governments were limited to police powers (e.g., protecting from rape and maintaining public decency), to the regulating of marriage and familial relations, and to the support and the protection of children and of families. Now, both federal and state governments are deeply involved with sex.

Once ostensibly excluded from the bedroom in the name of privacy by the courts, governmental agencies now seek control in the bedroom not only over our actions but over our thoughts as well. As but one example, the Health Systems Agencies Act (HSAA), which was passed in order to regulate the spending of public money in the building of hospitals and the purchasing of expensive medical equipment, has been used also to determine, by means of HSA-mandated state health-plans, the ways in which children shall be educated in matters of health—including sex education in accord with Planned Parenthood norms.

Public approval of the private conduct of those who sadly call themselves "gay"—not so private, however, that they do not want public knowledge and acceptance of their activities—has become a basic issue between major political parties.

Our government has for long years been sending abroad contraceptives and techniques of sterilization to the rest of the world; and its officials are on record saying that they would like to see at least a quarter of the fertile women of the world sterilized. Drugs too dangerous for American women are being sent, in contempt for those poorer than we, to women in developing nations. And abortion has often been forced on reluctant foreign governments in return for U.S. aid.

Few Americans realize how much the intellectual life of this nation has been guided, for at least a century and a half, by convinced atheists along a road, worse than any paganism, leading back into that darkness at the beginnings of our race where man freely chose to worship himself rather than God. That was the proto-sin, the sin of Adam. This has now been updated in modern versions, secular humanism and Marxism, the two great currents of thought growing out of the philosophies of the late 18th and early 19th centuries and summed up in the slogan of Feuerbach (whose most famous pupil was Karl Marx), "The only God of man is man himself." If people are brought, however subtly, to worship themselves, whether as individuals, through secular humanism, or as a group, through Marxism, then, indeed, confusion, chaos, and meaninglessness will take over not only in other areas but also in their sexual lives, as we can see all around us now.

Speaking of such philosophies, G. K. Chesterton remarked more than sixty years ago,

> According to most philosophers, God in making the world enslaved it. According to Christianity, in making it, He set it free. God

had written, not so much a poem, but rather a play; a play He had planned as perfect, but which had necessarily been left to human actors and stage-managers, who had since made a great mess of it.

Despite the "great mess" made of God's plan for human sexual activity, as for all else, He continues to direct His play and to lead it towards a successful conclusion. That we may share in His success, we need to learn what He is about, to understand what He has told us about our sexuality, so that we may indeed be free, free not with the sterile liberty of license and self-worship but with the freedom for which Christ has set us free, the freedom for which God created us—the freedom of His own children.

As Catholics, we are meant to be lights shining brightly in the darkness of surrounding sexual immorality. By the example of our chastity, by that puzzle and paradox which a chaste life represents in the eyes of those who do not believe, we are to bring people to Christ, who is the source of this chastity. Some of the things in our lives will be unique to Catholics, some will be simply the things that every man is called to by nature; in either case our witness can only ring true if we are indeed being chaste.

WHAT WE ARE LOOKING FOR

To live chastely, however, it is necessary to understand what chastity means for Christians. Why be chaste? Why is God interested in sex anyway?

We, who live in a country still influenced by Puritanism, even if only in reaction against it, have much need to be convinced of the true goodness of our bodies and especially of our own sexuality.

At times what prevents this conviction is that we fear our sexuality because of its violence and the ease with which it can get out of control; we sense its connection with original sin and our own actual sins; and we dread God's just punishment for the sins it may easily lead us to. At other times, we despise our sexual powers because they seem gross or dirty or, more subtly, because we find pleasure in them but no sense of true meaning, significance, or human worth.

But we forget, when we are afraid of our sexuality, that the best protection from sin in this matter is to revere and to esteem our sexuality as God reveres and esteems it. We forget, when we despise it, that it is God who has made our bodies to function in these ways, that it is He who has made us sexual beings and has filled the entire world with sexual beings. Yet, He intends for us to live in this world in a healthy, positive, holy, and Christian manner. Or we forget that the pleasure of sexual activity is intended by God only as an accompaniment to the achieving of its goals and true purposes or we are ignorant of its true significance for man.

We shall need to work a bit to obtain a sacred conviction in these matters because sexuality is so degraded all around us. Talk about sex nowadays is open, constant, and unembarrassed. But unfortunately this talk is, all too commonly, coarse and cheap; and men's actions are correspondingly coarse, cheap, and degraded. Sex has become mere pastime. The sexual organs are regarded by many as toys, simply for one's own pleasure. As a result, a great many people have no idea how good sex is. If you mention to them the sacredness of sex, they either take you to mean that sex is to be worshipped or else are puzzled and uncomprehending. No wonder they find no satisfaction in their sexual activities, no rest or peace, no matter how much they seek.

On the other hand, most of us have experienced the beauty of true chastity in some of the people we have met. It is obvious in them, not merely in the fact that they are not fooling around all the time but in a certain quality of character that is well summed up by St. Paul in his remarks to Timothy, "God has not given us a spirit of timidity, but of power, and love, and self-control." These three things:

power, love, and self-control, are probably the three best characteristics for describing Christian chastity. Certainly, they result from a chaste life.

Such chastity is our ideal. We are not interested in slipping into a state of repression, anxiety, fear, or constraints that cripple. Most of us have probably experienced some of these, too, at one time or another. It may even be said that they are necessary steps on the way to acquiring true chastity. Nonetheless, they are certainly not the goal.

As Christians, however, our goal is not chastity for its own sake. We are seeking, rather, to be like our Lord or our Lady. In the Bible, Mary is presented to us, when Gabriel speaks to her, as one who does not "know man," i.e., sexually, carnally. She has no intention of so knowing even Joseph, though well aware that such knowledge is necessary for the procreation of children. Our Lord, when He speaks in the Gospels about sexual matters, adultery, fornication, whatever, speaks in the same tone of voice, as far as we can judge, and with the same quiet seriousness that He does about any other moral matters. He does not make sex seem more important or more difficult or harder or scarier than anything else. Our question is: how do we come to His view of these things?

THE LIGHT OF CHRIST

Putting on the mind of Christ requires that we proceed in the light of faith, thinking of what God has revealed to us about Himself and about us. We wish to see what faith, our faith in Christ, implies for our behavior.

It has been argued by some theologians in recent times that, though the Church is able to define matters of faith, she cannot define moral matters. The reason they give is that morals are something other than faith and not deducible from it. Moral doctrine is in large measure culturally determined. It grows, they argue, from the circumstances of time and place as well as from one's personal devotion to Christ. Therefore, it is not something that can be solemnly defined for all times and places.

Unfortunately, such an argument would ultimately make Christian behavior not much different, indeed in principle no different, from that of the pagan. At most one might claim the Christian has better and more solid motives for carrying out the moral duties of his state. As the Council of Trent long since pointed out, however, faith and morals are not two distinct items. The Council stated its concern to be "with matters of faith and the morals that pertain to the upbuilding of the teaching of that faith." So, our concern here is with faith and the sexual behavior that flows from faith and in turn builds up the faith.

What, then, does faith teach about sexuality? Most obviously, that God created man male and female. But in that same passage there is something more pertinent and more fundamental: Man was created in the image and according to the likeness of God. Much later, St. Paul, when writing to the Colossians, says of Jesus, "He is the image of the invisible God, the first-born of all creation; in Him all things were created in heaven and on earth, visible and invisible .... All things were created through Him and for Him." Christ, then, is the image of God in which man was created. Jesus Christ, therefore, is the sole norm of what it is to be truly human, of what man is or is meant to be.

If, then, we wish to know the fullness of human good and not merely to inquire about those extreme moral evils that would destroy our nature, it is at Jesus and, in her measure, at Mary that we must look. He is the new Adam; she is the new Eve. In these two alone God's will for the human nature that He created can be seen whole and integral. If we look at human nature anywhere else, we are looking at a fallen nature. We can get a right picture of human sexuality—or anything else in our nature—only insofar as it is contained in Christ. In Him alone will we find unfallen human nature in its absolute fullness, as it was intended by God from the beginning.

It follows, since integral human nature is understandable only in Christ, that integral human sexuality is a mystery of faith. It is not merely something that we have in common with the animals though we share certain physiological aspects of sex with them. The mystery of man's sexuality is the mystery of its likeness to Christ's.

The whole of the natural law is summed up in Him. Rather, we should say, He *is* the natural law. His is our nature in its perfection. He is the norm for all that we do, think, or hope to be. It is Christ who sets all the questions and problems, contexts and answers; not we; not our sciences. The material universe was created through Him and for Him. He has come into it that He might bring it, in perfection and fulfillment, to the Father, even though, through sin, it had been delivered to slavery and death. For He loves all that He has made; and at the heart of the universe is the Heart of Christ.

If, then, we are to understand that part of the universe that is ourselves, and that aspect of ourselves that is our sexuality, we can do so only if we go to Christ. For, any truly human sexual behavior is essentially an element, aspect, or component of Christian chastity.

First, however, we shall pause to understand a little more deeply the goodness of the material world, sex included, and see how God uses material things to communicate with us through symbols. Thereafter, we will turn to the Scriptures to see what He has said there on our subject.

2

God's Good Creation: Christian Symbols

GOD AND MATTER

Unhealthy attitudes towards sexuality often spring from strong but hidden attitudes of disgust or dislike for our biological functions generally, our activity as material beings. Hence, before we begin to consider what God has revealed about sex, it may be helpful to look for a moment at God's attitude towards material things. The most obvious thing is that He likes them; He takes delight in them; He loves them.

Scripture recounts how God created the light, separating it from the darkness, created the sky and sea, then the land and its plant life, created the luminaries of the sky, the fish and the birds, the creeping things and the animals, and finally, man. The material universe, all parts and aspects of it without exception, was created by God; He looked at each thing as it came to be and "saw that it was good." All the while, the Bible adds, His Wisdom rejoiced, playing in this new-made world. God's attitude towards material things, then, is that of a maker well pleased with what he has made.

The one exception occurs when He made man. At the material level, man, too, was good; all his spiritual powers were good, but these were capable of being used or misused. So God waits before saying that man is either good or bad. Because He has given man the great gift of freedom, in likeness to Himself, He waits to see what man is going to do with his freedom. God has left man unfinished so that he can become like God even in His act of creation, creating himself by the gift of God's grace, through his own free actions.

Christianity, therefore, differs greatly from the old nature-religions of the Near East, of Babylonia, Egypt, and elsewhere. We know, as they did not, that there can be no evil in God. Since God is the sole source of all that is, nothing else exists for a creature to be modeled on or to be like except the infinite goodness of God. Hence, there is no evil in His creation except what His creatures bring about by abusing their freedom. Matter is good; it is not, as Hinduism and other major Oriental religions have thought, ambivalent or bad, a sort of cosmic illusion or force for evil embedded in the structure of the universe. Quite the contrary, the whole of creation is good; everything that exists is something that God wants to exist. As a wise man said in prayer to the Lord, "You love all things that are, and You loathe nothing of the things You have made." (*Wis* 11:24-25).

Still more striking is the fact that God has taken up the material elements of this world into Himself. By His enfleshment (the literal sense of the Latin term "incarnation"), He took up a human body, as material as ours, with flesh and blood and all the biological structures and functions of our bodies. He makes this human animality one with Himself, so that we must say of this particular man, Jesus Christ, "This human being, material though He is, is God." The eternal Word has become flesh forever. There is never a time this will cease to be true, now that it has once happened. We should let this sink into us because it is basic for everything that we will say.

Christians sometimes fail to realize the importance that Scripture gives to Christ's body, His own physical body, not just His mystical body. Firstly, we have been redeemed and have been sanctified through the offering of the body of Jesus Christ once and for all upon the cross. Only a material being can be scourged and crucified. Only in a body capable, like ours, of sensation and of pain, could the infinitely spiritual God suffer, bleed, and die for our sins.

Furthermore, we were justified by the raising of His flesh and blood in glory from the tomb, by the new life of that body that had died for us on the cross. His entrance into heaven was a bodily entrance. Christ's resurrection and ascension are, then, the ultimate proof of the goodness of material things, of man's body and of all the material creation which assists man.

This bodily glorification of Christ is the seed and root of our salvation and our glorification. We are called by Christ to do in our bodies as He did in His body: to suffer, to die, and to rise in glory in our own flesh, made glorious by the power of His Spirit.

This is the reason why He gives us His body as nourishment when we receive Him in Communion. It is the body of the Risen One that we receive. Looking and tasting to us now like bread and wine, yet it has the same powers that it had right after His resurrection. The apostles were gathered together, the doors were shut, and Christ, body and whole being, was suddenly present. He willed to be there; there He was. So He does at Mass, in Communion, in the tabernacle—He is present because He has chosen to come there upon the altar when the priest consecrates. Though capable of multi-location and movement as fast as thought, Christ's body is still a human body; it is still flesh and blood, though glorified with powers that our bodies as yet do not know, but will some day have. His is also the body of the sacrifice that is offered; His is the body of the priest, for it is He who offers Himself upon the altar to the Father.

St. Paul, all through his Epistles, never ceases to talk about the body of Christ, the flesh of Christ, the blood of Christ. He says very little, if anything, about the soul of Christ. Obviously, he speaks of the *living* body of Christ, alive by the life of His soul. But it is the *body* of Christ that is the center of his thought. All our hope centers on His body, e.g., when He returns at the end of time as Judge. Dominated by this mystery of the body of Christ as the source of salvation, Paul's preferred image of the Church is that of the mystical body of Christ, His material extension in space and in time.

The body of the one who is closest to Christ, Mary's body, completes the mystery. In 1950, Pope Pius XII defined solemnly the doctrine of the assumption of our Lady, body and soul, into the glory of heaven. This doctrine emphasizes for us something that we might have forgotten in connection with Christ Himself: that those who rise from the dead rise as male or female. Mary remains woman; she remains "she"; she remains female for all eternity, even as her Son is a man, "He," male forever.

Though flesh and blood, in the scriptural sense of human weakness, cannot inherit the kingdom of God, flesh and blood made glorious by their link with Christ's flesh and blood *do* inherit the kingdom. We will all be in heaven more truly male or female than ever on this earth, without marriage, but perfect in virility or femininity for all ages.

CHRISTIAN SYMBOLISM

Of course, Christ, Mary, and the rest of us, are not just material; we are spiritual as well. Our activities are at once bodily and intellectual, freely chosen and materially determined. Our thoughts, our emotions, our freedom, our passions, our digestion, and our sexuality are inseparably welded together in one, single being. It is this strange sort of material-spiritual composite that God loves so much. Because He made us, He never forgets (though we often do) the sort of composite creatures we are; and He deals with us accordingly.

Thus, the greatest of His spiritual gifts He gives through largely material means. Our share in His divine life, exercised through faith, hope, and charity, is spiritual beyond any human notion of spirituality. Nonetheless, this is given to us in the sacraments through concrete material things such as water, bread, wine, olive oil, and balsam. Recall the catechism definition of a sacrament: an outward sign (in other words, a material thing) of an interior grace, established by Christ and conferring the grace which (as a material thing) it signifies, i.e., some new mode or way of living the supernatural life of grace or some new growth in it. Materiality enters into the very notion of what a sacrament is. Means of grace, yes; but it gives this grace through matter, by showing forth to our senses some likeness and similarity to a mystery on the spiritual level. A sign of this type is called a "symbol."

A symbol is, first, a type of material thing that, when perceived, leads us to a knowledge of something else. It is, therefore, a type of sign. Some signs are purely conventional, words for example—whether spoken or written. When I say "fire," this means something in English; it would mean nothing at all in French. It is a sign that leads you to a knowledge of my meaning when I use the word in a sentence, but only if you already know what its conventional signification is. Further, the word itself will not help you to learn its meaning. The word "fire" designates a certain kind of physico-chemical process but bears no resemblance to that process.

A sign, however, may resemble what it signifies. If, in this case, both sign and thing signified are material, the sign is called an image. Thus, a painting of blazing logs in a fireplace would offer us an image of fire.

But the material sign that we call a symbol has a sign-value not only by some sort of convention or by material similarity but by the fact that its material form, structure, action, or appearance is similar to or like the immaterial or spiritual thing it signifies. Hence, once we know that something is a symbol, it can lead us by itself to knowledge of its significance and meaning.

For example, fire is widely used as a symbol of human love. Fire is bright and beautiful. It is mobile and active, spreading and growing as if alive. It warms us and gives heat. It is necessary for civilized life; without it we cannot cook our food, keep warm in winter, or melt metals out of the rock. Yet, if fire gets out of control, it becomes something terrible, destructive, leaving only ashes. So it is with human love. Love brightens our lives and warms our hearts. It turns the indigestible events and tasteless dreariness of everyday life into true nourishment. Love will draw joy and benevolence from hearts of stone. With little love, life is cold and painful; with none at all, life is impossible. Yet, if love once gets out of control, it consumes, destroys all in its way, and leaves only ashen desolation. Fire in its different physical aspects, then, is like love in its immaterial aspects. Material fire leads us to a knowledge of love's "fire" by summing up and making manifest to the senses our own inner experience of love.

Many symbols flow from similarities almost universally observed and noticed, as in our example of fire and love. Many others are more strongly conditioned by the particular experiences of peoples or cultures. A man's aggressiveness, for example, chooses different types of symbolic action to express itself in different cultures. In our culture, it can show itself by bigness—owning the largest ranch, building the biggest factory, producing the most steel—or by excellence in sports. In other cultures, aggressiveness is manifested in the number of wives in a harem or by the number of children born, by heads or scalps collected, by grave risks taken or perils confronted, or in the various forms of male contest.

Human cultures, our own and others, are in large measure summed up by their symbols. One of the symbols of our own culture is the skyscraper. Recall people's reactions when a new building is put up that is taller than any other, e.g., the Empire State Building in New York or the Sears Tower in Chicago. Such a building has a meaning and we know it, even if we find it hard to state explicitly what the meaning is exactly. The solid gold Cadillac is a symbol with which we are all acquainted. So is the man in the gray flannel suit (and the blue-jeans generation) and the various status symbols. All these are purely material and external things—clothing, articles of manufacture—yet in the context of our culture, they sum up a whole range of social relationships by their physical similarity to the attitudes they signify.

At a deeper level, psychologists are coming to understand the psychological role of symbolism in man's life. They have discovered that, long before an infant is capable of speech, before he is capable of expressing anything, we would think, except by crying and wailing, he has begun to use symbols. As soon as he becomes aware of his bodily functions, he uses them for symbolic acts of love, rejection, and aggression. All man's sexual activity, as we shall see in detail, is symbolic activity. We have mentioned the range of aggressive symbols, some of which are subdued to social goods, but others not. Most of what we call culture—art, literature, and even science—is composed and built up of symbols. Politicians are well aware of the benign paternity expressed by kissing a baby or the fraternal goodwill embodied in a handshake and use of the first name.

Finally, there are levels of symbolism of which ordinarily we are not conscious at all. Much of the work of Freud, Jung, and of other depth-psychiatrists has been to lay bare these hidden structures of symbolism that lie far down within us, of which we are not conscious, but which, nonetheless, work actively upon our motivation without our realizing their hidden biases.

The psychiatrists were interested because they had seen the enormous damage that can be done to a person if these deep symbolic structures are skewed or damaged or wrongly related to reality. In such a case, a man is at odds with himself or the world. What was created in him to symbolize one thing, has been made to symbolize something else. The result can easily be psychosis.

Symbols, then, some of them conscious, others not, but all important, are continually at work within us. Many symbols, indeed, flow from man's very nature; and man cannot distort or change them without doing damage to himself. Symbolism belongs to the very essence of man, a necessary aspect of his being.

Returning to sacramental symbols, consider baptism. This involves immersing a person in a pool or tank of water, though this act is often reduced to a pouring of water over the person's head. But what does water symbolize? Universally, it is found to be a symbol of life. For, every living thing needs water to continue its life. Without it we die in the terrible agony of thirst. With it, even in the deserts, plants germinate and cacti bloom.

At the same time it symbolizes death, because if we are plunged into water and our heads held under, we shortly lose consciousness and drown. Water in excess becomes the floodwaters that sweep away life from the surface of the land, yet render it fertile for new life to spring up. Water, then, kills; it also gives life. Immersion symbolizes death; coming up out of water, life. Thus Christ chose to plunge us into water to symbolize our death with Him on the cross to our old selves and to the world, and to lift us out of water to symbolize our being raised to a new life in Him through His resurrection.

Not only are all the sacraments symbolic but the entire liturgy is saturated with symbols. In fact, the liturgy can be defined quite usefully as a series of symbolic actions through which man worships God and through which God's grace is given to man. The altar itself, the priest's gestures, the types of readings, the way we listen to the readings—sitting during the Old-Testament reading and the New-Testament letters but standing for the Gospel—the carrying of candles, the offering of incense, the bread and the wine themselves, the chalice, . . . an endless list of symbolic elements, all fitting to form the one sacrifice and the one banquet of Christ.

But the liturgy contains much more than rites and ceremonies. The liturgy re-enacts symbolically the great mysteries of God's actions in history. For example, baptism represents God's freeing of His people from their slavery in Egypt by their passage through the Red Sea dry-shod while their enemies drowned in the waters, prefiguring His liberating us from the power of Satan through the waters of baptism. So also, the Mass is a rich symbolic re-presentation of the whole history of the Jewish people and of God's relations with them and all mankind, from the first offering of the paschal lamb in Egypt to the sacrifice of the Lamb of God on the cross to take away the sin of the world, the sacrifice that incorporates and transcends all other sacrifices. Sacrifice itself, of course, is a type of symbolic action reserved exclusively for man's worship of God.

The Paschal Liturgy carries this symbolism to its highest point. It should cause no surprise that the Church splurges on symbolism at this time of the year in her joy at Christ's bodily resurrection, stressing in this way that the whole material creation is good and intended for the service and glory of the Father. There are not only the usual symbols to which we have grown accustomed—altar, candles, chalice, paten, music, incense, flowers—but there is a vast array of special ones. All the lights in the church are turned out, to remind us of the darkness of our sins. There is the entrance of the Paschal candle; and the light coming from that candle, as the feeble flames are passed from one person to another, like the graces of faith and conversion. Palm branches, processions, breathings upon the water in the baptismal font, the consecrating and pouring of oils, the washing of feet, the consecrating of fire—these and many other symbols are crammed into one short week; most of them, into a single night.

It is right here, in its attitude towards symbols, that we find a tremendous difference between Catholicism and all the types of puritanism or so-called "religion of the spirit," which are such perpetual temptations to many people. The latter may, indeed, use many symbols; but they do so in a strangely minimalistic fashion, using symbols that are as abstract as possible, mere wraiths or ghosts of Catholic symbols. For Catholicism is of the earth, earthly; as well as of heaven, heavenly. We see that material things are not only good but useful; not only for man's benefit and pleasure but for his service to God, even in the highest and most exalted moments of his religious life.

Thus, the whole life of the Church is symbolic, not only sacraments and worship but, as we shall now see, divine revelation and all morality. If, then, we do not understand symbolism, we will have but small understanding of Christianity.

SYMBOLS IN REVELATION

In the light of God's use of sacramental symbols to share with us His own life, it will be no surprise to find that His revelation of Himself to us through the Scriptures also makes heavy use of symbols.

We ourselves, as material-and-spiritual composites, find it particularly easy and attractive to communicate with each other by means of symbols. It is true that the most characteristically human mode of communication takes place through words, which are non-symbolic signs. But we have many symbolic ways of communicating also. Perhaps the commonest of these go today under the name "body-language." Surely, a mother's caress of her infant or the studied casualness of a self-conscious young man at a party portray for us in flesh their inner attitudes and feelings. Often, too, when we do use words, we use them in order to represent a symbol that we cannot present in actuality.

Since symbolic communication is part of our nature,

especially at the deepest levels, God has used symbolism to communicate with us, to reveal Himself to us, and to teach us more about ourselves. The mere fact that He has done so sharpens our awareness that man is a symbol-making animal, a creature that lives his life in the power of symbols. God, having created us this way, speaks to us in the language that is best suited to us—and this is often the language of symbols.

When we read in the Scriptures the history of our salvation, we find that both Testaments are so heavily crammed with symbolism that they often make extremely difficult reading. At times, the symbolism seems to get totally out of hand, as in *Ezekiel* or in *Apocalypse* and we are tempted to say, "Well, we'll reserve that for another time." But even in the parts of Scripture given over, seemingly, to simple narrative, such as the Gospels, we find abundant symbolism. For example, St. John's gospel is contructed precisely to show the symbolic value that is present in the actual, historical deeds and words of Christ.

Why this profusion of symbolism? One reason is that God wished to save, to fulfill, and to bring to completion all the good that was already in man. Now, throughout the whole course of history, religion had been, more than any other single aspect of man's life, the strongest focus of his symbolic activity. Thus, one reason God revealed Himself to us was to rectify the skewed symbolic activity which constitutes so much of natural human religions. Even the highest of these, such as Hinduism or Buddhism, are in many ways profoundly in error; and these errors generate false attitudes towards the world and other men, which are propagated through their religious symbols.

If, then, God was to redeem us fully, He had to set right our religious symbols. He could not obliterate symbolic action, for this would be to obliterate our nature. So He took the symbolisms that we are acquainted with, which He had built into us and our world, even though they were badly damaged by sin. He took these, rectified them, and reoriented them. Through these restored symbolisms, He has enabled us to have a right understanding of the material universe and has revealed to us the true meaning of man.

A second reason is that God wishes to tell us things that lie beyond the range of comprehension of even the highest of our intellectual powers. He wishes to give us true knowledge of Himself, of His own internal life as Trinity, of the incarnation, and of all the other mysteries of the faith, far beyond human understanding. Great as is the human mind, it is still infinitely weaker than is necessary to get a proper grasp of God Himself or of His mysteries.

On the other hand, a symbol, because of its concreteness, contains within itself tremendous potentialities that the mind cannot exhaust. This is especially true of natural symbols, because God Himself created the material universe to show forth the spiritual; and, as we said above, there is nothing else, ultimately, for any material thing to be like other than God. Thus, sheep were created, among other reasons, that Christ might be the Lamb of God; lions, that He might be the Lion of the tribe of Judah.

Though these symbols, also, are not adequate to contain God's mysteries, yet by His creating them thus, they are better far than our limited concepts and thought-patterns. This we see easily from the fact that theologians have been pondering the revealed symbolisms for centuries and have found ever new and true, though previously hidden, meanings there.

A final reason is that God wished His revelation to transcend all time, place, and culture because He wants to speak to every man so that He can be understood. Since a single symbol can pack a richness of meaning far exceeding the grasp of any one time, place, or culture, God can reveal things to us through symbols that lie beyond particular cultural conditionings. Since symbols touch the nature of man in the depths of his unconscious, they are able to speak to him universally, even when he is without education.

We may distrust symbols because we think of them

chiefly as signs that are artful or contrived. "Symbol" is often used loosely, and may refer to nothing more than some bit of "inspired prose" or, say, a movie's cheap way of manipulating emotions by paralleled images. Men easily find this sort of symbolism faintly embarrassing because, I think, it seems feminine to them. In fact, women seem generally to find the concreteness and emotional directness of symbols more satisfying than men do, who miss the abstract generality and rigorous clarity of conceptual thought. Men can forget, consequently, their own experience and the things psychology has shown us; they tend to hold back in the presence of symbolic activity, not to enter into it, to feel just a little bit silly if they do engage in it.

We distrust symbols also because they can be abused. A symbol has meaning; its meaning arises from the sort of thing it is. Like a word, it can be used by one person to express his meaning to another; it can be used as a part of a language. When it is so used, it should mean to the persons involved that which it does mean in itself. But people can use a symbol falsely. While pretending to all the world that they mean what the symbol expresses, at the same time they are intending something quite different. In other words, they lie. Unfortunately, the symbols proper to every human relationship can be violated and used contrary to their meaning; such symbolism has then become a mere vehicle for hypocrisy.

Consequently, we can be either bored by symbols or sickened by them when they are abused. This is, however, only an argument for using them well, an argument for studying and understanding them more deeply. We will, therefore, be discussing in the rest of this book, Christian sexual symbolism: first, the natural symbolism of the body and of the marital act, then the further meaning of sexual actions that is made known to us in and through the Scriptures, then the meanings of corruptions of these symbolic acts, and finally the symbolism of continence and virginity.

3

Sexual Intercourse: The Natural Word of Love

We have seen that God communicates with us through symbols, partly spiritual and partly material, in correspondence with our nature. Now we wish to consider the natural symbolism of sexual intercourse itself, that is, to learn those meanings that even people without revelation can come to know, meanings that God built into these physical acts through internal likeness and parallelism of structure. We will then be better able to understand the supernatural meanings God reveals to us when He uses symbols in Scripture.

Most obviously, sexual actions symbolize love. But, the love so symbolized is not love-in-general. There are many types of love which are not sexual, in any popular sense of the term, and not related directly to sexual activity, e.g., the love of a son for his father or of a daughter for her mother, the love of a brother for a brother, of one friend for another, and all types of civic love. None of these loves is sexual, in the sense of drawing to genital arousal and intimacy, whereas marital love is deeply sexual. Yet even marital love has many varieties and modes of expression other than sexual intimacies or intercourse.

Well, then, what kind of love *is* symbolized by sexual action? To answer, we must note that even the way our bodies are formed sexually has meaning that lies beyond the physical. Our bodies are not mere collections of functions, but express visibly part of the natural and intrinsic meaning of our selves.

THE MEANING OF THE BODY

Consider a man's body. His genitals are external, hanging loosely from his body. On arousal, they point away from him and, at climax, expel his seed from him. He responds quickly to visual stimuli. The mere sight of a woman, especially if he senses that she is interested in him, can arouse him at once sexually. His sexual response is quick and strong; his whole body reacts rapidly. He can cease to act, cease even to be stimulated, with equal rapidity, especially if some other stimulus, say, an intrusion by a burglar, calls for immediate but different action.

Hence, a man has great freedom with regard to sexual activity. He can initiate it rapidly; he can stop it abruptly. After-effects are minimal or nonexistent. He can begin intercourse and carry it to completion even against the wishes of the woman. He can coerce a woman, rape her if he should so desire.

What all this signifies to him symbolically is not hard to fathom. As his genitals and his actions through them are largely external and outwardly directed, so at the pyschic level he is directed outward and focuses his interest spontaneously on things outside himself. Even as his arousal and orgasm tend to be quick and soon over, so on the psychological level he tends to action rather than simple contemplation of what attracts him. As his sexual activity is aggressive, so he is interested in display and in manifestation of his sexuality, if not directly, then in contest against other men. And the whole of his life manifests his inner need to take initiative.

Because of this highly external and other-directed genitality, a man's family remains in large measure psychologically external to him. His sexual independence and freedom of action signify a corresponding psychic independence and freedom with regard to his family. He may father more than one family; he may sire offspring whose existence is of small concern to him. The family is part of his life, but not the totality of it. The family extends him in space and time, in range of influence and power, and is able to give him a type of support and assistance that the rest of society cannot provide but often makes necessary.

Correspondingly, he will establish very strong relationships with the world lying beyond both himself and his family. Always he senses a duty to act in the world at large, to make full and proper use of his powers in whatever field of activity he lives and operates. He is one who builds in the world.

A man's interiority, consequently, is that which comes from the mind. It is through the mind that he grasps the external world, grasps even his own feelings and his own sexuality, for that matter. For, once he has reached adulthood, however pleasant his feelings or emotions, he is not satisfied until his mind has understood them and traced them. And through this interiority of the mind, he is then able to build, to construct, to make the world a suitable place for himself and his family. Thus, a man is largely verbal and conceptual, using his mind to obtain understanding and, so, to affect the world.

On the other hand, he is also expendable. His body is made both for dangerous actions and for quick reaction in response to danger. He can fertilize many women, one after another, so that if one man is left with a thousand women, he is capable of generating children of all of them. Society does not need an individual man, then, the way it needs each individual woman. It can afford to send men into battle to protect, even at the cost of their lives, the women and children at home.

A woman's body is very different. Her genitals are interior, hidden. Her response is largely tactile. Mere seeing does little to arouse her; touch does a great deal. A woman's response is much slower than a man's. She is not only slower to be aroused, she is slower in subsiding; and many a marital problem comes from the fact that the husband, having subsided quickly from his sexual excitement, turns away and pays no further attention to his wife though she is still fully aroused.

This prolongation of the effects of intercourse within her body signifies an even greater prolongation in her mind and emotions. And if she conceives, for long months she will be heavy with child, thus beginning a relation with that child that the father can never have.

In order that a child may grow within her body, there is an empty space within her that only another person can fill. Yet she will not know him until he is born. Because of this inner space, open for the mystery of new persons, a woman's interiority is not primarily of the mind, brilliant though her mind may be, but is rooted in her womb and its openness for the seed of her husband and for a child.

Sensing the child as the desired filling of that central emptiness that must otherwise remain part of her, a woman is led to find that missing center in a family, and her fulfilment in the raising of children who will be worthy of her love. Thus, she is not greatly concerned with the abstract class of beings that consitute the not-yet-materialized needs, hazards, and threats that the man must deal with if he is to preserve his family in a world that is not easily made subservient to their welfare. Rather, her attention is focused on the concrete being within her and upon her other children, already born, around her.

This explains something of a woman's special power of nonverbal communication. She must be able to understand her newborn infant and respond appropriately to his needs. She must reassure, encourage, and assist this helpless creature who cannot speak, who for a year or more will not be able to communicate with her by words.

Even when she is not pregnant, a woman does not ordinarily have the bodily strength to resist a man successfully if he is determined to rape her or to kill her children. Her efforts to repel him, however savage or frantic, are concentrated on protection and defense; she lacks the man's aggressive strength. Though willing to give her life, if need be, to save her children from attack, frequently she has not the power to do so. She needs someone who can protect both her and the family her life centers on.

This bodily weakness with regard to conflict and assault grounds a woman's greater fearfulness or sensitivity to danger and signifies her psychic need for security. Without the latter, even her physical fertility, by nature intermittent, is further reduced. But when secure, the woman nourishes her child with the milk from her own breasts; and a nursing mother is that which a man must protect above all else.

Nor is it strange that the protection a culture offers to its women and to their children, gathered about them or still within their womb, is the sign of its vitality. The preservation and transmission of culture seem to be universally symbolized by the infant at its mother's breast, by the children at her knee. For she is called by her nature to nourish them spiritually as well as physically. As her body needs more and better food when nursing, so children turn her mind to draw in all of the more stable and contemplative aspects of the culture, to digest them, and transmit them in forms suitable to her children.

Thus, all that the past has brought forth, as from a womb—language (one's "mother-tongue"), stories (the concrete historical memory), arts and literature, and domestic skills—she takes in and, through her ability as first teacher of her children, serves as the cultural memory of the entire people. The father, on the other hand, more naturally teaches the culture's abstract understanding of its own socio-political nature and of the world as a whole, along with those active skills more useful outside, even if for, the family. He is more at ease in training young adults to labor at generating the future, to lay bare by intellectual analysis the possibilities of the world, and to risk the dangers involved in bringing them to be.

At the highest level, then, a woman's bodily unsuitability for combat symbolizes her basic drive for commitment, a desire and a need for love and, in a certain way, for guidance by the man she loves and trusts. Men, outwardly directed, see their responsibilities to their families as met in large measure by their efforts to attain certain societal goals they have set for themselves. Made to take initiative in the world, yet in such a way as to promote the good of their family, they know a basic need to have and exercise authority, in the world perhaps, but especially over their family, so as to hold the inner and outer portions of their life in unity. But, spurred by ambition and concentrating on personal achievement as measured by their goals, men have a natural tendency to avoid marital commitment as not always helpful to these goals, if not an actual entanglement or impediment to them.

Thus, it is clear how fully in accord with our nature are St. Paul's commands, "Husbands, love your wives" (Eph.5:25,28,33; Col.3:19); and "Wives, be subject to your husbands" (Eph.5:22,24,33; Col.3:18). The man who truly loves his wife satisfies her greatest need as a woman, her need for the security of a steadfast love and faithful protection. The wife who obeys her husband confirms the need he has for authority so that he can accept his full responsibility towards his family. She thus helps him to hold fast to a commitment he might otherwise be tempted to reject; whereas a wife who disregards her husband's authority robs him of his function and undermines his ability to give her what she most needs and desires, his abiding love. So, too, the husband who is not concerned to make manifest in body, mind, and heart his love for his wife, makes it far harder for her to submit to his authority, no longer seen as being exercised for her good but arbitrarily or merely for others. He thus weakens her ability to give him that support, in his wrestling with the world, that he needs from her.

There are many other things our bodies symbolize antecedently to the dynamic of the marital union. Let us glance at one, less obvious, symbolism that Pope John Paul II has analyzed at great length: the symbolism of the physical nakedness of husband and wife in each other's presence.

We find this first in the Garden of Eden, where man and wife, as first created, were both naked; yet they were not ashamed. Physical nakedness seems at first easy to define. It is the lack of all clothing, all covering, all protection, all that is not the person himself or herself. Thus, when two are present to each other, it is the exposure of one's whole body to another's gaze, scrutiny, and judgment, without anything that can enhance, screen, or protect.

Nakedness before another is more than mere nudity, however, for it symbolizes that each is meant to be uncovered to the other spiritually. This does not mean confessing prior infidelities or other sins to one another— for this tends, generally, to be an obstacle to transparency. It means rather that each stands in the present moment without psychological covering or pretense, in the presence of the other. Neither spiritually, mentally, emotionally, nor physically is one covering or concealing any of one's interior self. And each accepts the other, seen thus naked, whatever defects are thus exposed.

In a state of original innocence, one could stand so, in front of one's husband or wife, without any trace of shame. As Christians in a fallen world, we are constantly being recalled by our Lord and His Church to that state.

But in our fallen state, nakedness before another calls, especially in a woman, for no small trust and humility. Will her husband accept her for herself, as she is in herself, regardless of any imperfection, fault, or flaw, whether physical or spiritual?

In turn, the husband must be able to give himself to her as he is in his masculinity, without pretending to be less or more than he is. Only through her can he discover what it is to be a man, to be truly male. Each of them stands as a personal gift from God before the other. Hence, each is not only to revere and appreciate the other but to worship God through the other, because it is He who has given the gift.

THE MEANING OF INTERCOURSE

In sexual intercourse itself, the man takes the initiative, but in response to the physical presence and attraction of the woman. She responds to his arousal by her own. As he penetrates, she opens and yields herself to him, permitting him to take possession of her. Letting him act, she also acts to draw his seed from him. He labors and thrusts upon and in her, in order to pour into her his semen.

The fullness of intrinsic symbolic meaning in intercourse is seen from the fact that any such description of the physical act can be read, with scarcely a change, as a description of the couple's psychic activity. The man's initiative and the woman's opening are not merely physical but also psychological. The man's dominance in penetrating and taking possession is an attitude of mind and heart, not mere bodily power. The woman's gift of herself to the man, his gift of himself to her, are spiritual and psychological as well as physical. His aggressive giving of his substance to her, her yielding of her substance, hidden deep within, to him, describe spiritual realities no less than biological ones.

The woman shows submission and responsiveness, an unfolding, a centering of her attention upon him. She seeks, as an abiding psychological attitude, to draw forth what is best in him, not just from his body but from all levels of his being. Likewise, when the man penetrates her, he focuses all of his activity, all of his substance, all of his responsibility, all of his manhood upon her. He is fascinated with her; he desires to protect her. In his case, also, these are meant to be abiding attitudes.

The most obvious aspect of sexual union is the pleasure it gives. But even this physical delight, though so strongly and intensely felt in the flesh, symbolizes something beyond itself. For the pleasure one receives, as also the pleasure that one gives, is a pleasure that comes from, through, and by another person.

The fact that intercourse is with another person gives rise, of course, to the greatest pleasures in marriage. One is filled with joy as a newly-wed, for example, at being received by the person one most loves and respects precisely in and through one's sexual organs and powers. What was before, if not shameful, at least ambiguous, is now validated and made in the strongest sense acceptable. One's sexual desires and activity are now known as good, not merely in an intellectual way but through one's own experience of the beloved's pleasure produced by one's own sexual initiative or response. One's pleasure, then, is not an isolated pleasure centered on one's own body, validating nothing and generating shame. It is a pleasure of mind and heart in which the pleasure of another becomes one's own.

Yet, given our weakness, this interpersonal aspect imposes what we sense as limitations or constraints upon us. There are times we would desire to do things that, at least under the circumstances, should not be done. Or there are things that, little as we feel like it at the moment, we ought to do. For, this person is not simply an object that one is dealing with—an object being by definition something one can take total possession of and use as he wishes, whatever the effects on the object. The beloved is another person, of equal rights and stature, of equal dignity before God. Hence, one is not free to use him or her for one's pleasure—or other purposes—nor even as one upon whom pleasure may be imposed. Any attempt, obviously, to force the other person sexually contradicts the signification of this built-in "limitation" on intercourse that is constituted by the other person.

But there is another aspect of interpersonal limitation upon intercourse. No man is capable of giving all of himself to his wife. Even if he could, he may not do so; he belongs to God. Similarly, no woman may give all of herself to her husband. Neither owns himself. They love each other, they are bound to each other; but only God truly possesses either or can claim the total love of either. Total union with one who is not God is impossible. And were it possible, it would be idolatry, giving the creature the status of the divine. And on the other hand, only God can own and take total possession of any person without destroying or degrading that person.

Two human creatures, then, can never be so united that they are only one, something that appears symbolically from the very fact that the two bodies cannot melt into one another as they imagine at times they desire to do. Any attempt to go beyond this limit produces only pain and agony.

This physical separateness-in-union acts as a symbol of what occurs at the psychic level. In the very act of intercourse itself there arises the realization that each is alone even when most intimately united with the other. The love one seeks to express is known, in the very expressing of it, to be inadequate. No love of a creature can take the place of the love of God. This aloneness, then, is itself a symbol of an openness to God—not merely as the agent who may create on this occasion another human being but as the only one who can truly satisfy one's love. Through the other person, one is invited to love God more deeply and more perfectly.

It is not that one should love the other person less in order to love God more; rather, just because one loves God more, one loves more all those He loves. Indeed, the richness of God's infinite love makes up for and compensates for our own lack of goodness. One's partner is always a limited human being, who may not be able or willing to give the pleasures one desires to have or even to receive the pleasures one desires to give. And honesty compels the same admission of oneself. But knowing that God alone can satisfy all our desires, we can the more easily bear with these limitations that serve to remind us of the Center of all love.

This physical act of union, however, remains always the symbolic expression of the desire for an ever deeper emotional and spiritual oneness with each other. Now, biologically, intercourse can, and frequently does, result in the fusion of the male principle with the female. When the act has thus its total consequences, a new human person comes into being. This fusion of the two principles is a further intensification of the union of the two partners in one single flesh, the flesh of their child. At the same moment, as a union which they make possible but do not control, it signifies their subordination of themselves as parents to the growth and development of the child.

The child's symbolizing of its parents' union has yet another aspect, one of anticipation and the desire to make one's partner a parent. Though intense in many cultures, including that of biblical Israel, this desire is much muted in our culture. Rarely strong, it is often not only absent but repudiated—with immeasurable loss for society as well as for individuals. Yet the symbolism remains, no less than the reality: the mystery of parenthood, which offers new strength and maturity to the personality of each and without which neither can realize all his natural potential. The fullness of bodily union continues to signify that fullness of mutual love which seeks the other's sexual perfecting through parenthood.

A wife desires, at least on the symbolic level, to give her husband the fullness of manhood, the gravity, the dignity, the sense of responsibility and sobriety which characterize a father. The husband in turn desires, as Abraham did for Sarah, to give his wife that particular richness, warmth, and fierce tenderness which are characteristic of a mother.

This union of man and woman, though so private in act, is manifested and made public through their children. A child is not merely conceived; it is to be nurtured and educated to take its place in the world. The parents' surrender and self-giving in sexual union, then, as ordered toward maturation and perfecting through children, both symbolizes and effects the whole communal structure of human society, built up through familial relationships into ever higher-level communities. Precisely as generative, moreover, sexual intercourse manifests the community of the successive generations of mankind, the common bonds that unite the children of Adam throughout all ages.

It is not surprising, then, that in no societies, save those decaying in the last stages of individualism, has marriage been considered a private affair. Everywhere it has been subject to social regulation and control. The private will of two people has never been adequate, by itself, to validate their union, whatever their love for one another.

In this context too, the limitations of the physical act are symbolic. Sexual intercourse is not in itself an act creative of a child; it is only procreative. Each parent contributes, from his own biological substance, to that unique and single gift which God may use for the creation of a new human person. But since the parents are not the creators of their child, they do not own it, just as they do not own each other.

Thus, a sort of adoption must take place, a fact which is the ultimate basis for adoption in its ordinary sense. The adopted child, it is true, has genetic materials not found in its adoptive parents, and thus has a material substrate more different from theirs and from their natural children's than these from one another. But, as a human person, the adopted child is no further from these adoptive parents than their natural offspring are.

NATURAL MARRIAGE

All these things, and many others, are said simply by the act of intercourse itself. It is a rare human being, however, who is going to understand, realize, and appreciate all of these things, especially when they are as young as most people are when they marry. The meaning of marital union, of which we have only glimpsed a bit, is too rich for a young person just entering marriage to understand it fully.

Nonetheless, he can know that some such richness of meaning is present. He can begin to see something of it, enough to desire it and to strive to turn this objective symbol which is his sexual union with his wife or hers with her husband, into a word of love. Intercourse is meant to become a type of language by which husband and wife are able to express to each other all that they wish to say in the way of love and spiritual union.

To make this meaning fully one's own, one has to learn what that meaning is. The desire to do so, so as to be able to speak well this word of love, grounds the institution of marriage. Marriage, then, is the institution by which those who do not yet know how to say totally by their act of sexual intercourse all that sexual intercourse means bind themselves to live in such a way as to achieve that knowledge and understanding and to grow through practice into expressing in each marital act what are, at that moment, the most appropriate aspects, if not the totality, of that meaning.

Human beings are imperfect. Such an ideal will never be fully realized in this life. Nonetheless, the direction is clear and, through meeting and talking with older people who have been married for long years, one sees that the ideal can be well approximated. Because of just this imperfection, natural marriage is, with some qualifications, indissoluble. It cannot be broken up or dissolved, because there is no defect of love whatever that can invalidate a solemn contract to overcome all of one's defects of love and to assist in all ways possible one's spouse to do the same. The ground for entering into this union is precisely the knowledge that both are defective in love's perfection, and that neither person is as yet able to intend fully what his body is already saying by the act of intercourse.

Whatever the other person's faults, then, they are always to be dealt with in love, tender or stern as the situation requires. But it is precisely to this love that one commits oneself by marriage.

Saying all this, of course, is much easier than doing it; and marriage requires great self-sacrifice. This is not to deny that intercourse is a healing balm emotionally for the inevitable minor irritations of early marriage while two people are attempting the difficult task of oneness in spirit, mind, and heart. Coming together in body presupposes and invites to forgiveness of the small offenses that are the residue of the self-sufficiency that has ruled prior to marriage.

But not all is that simple. One is forced to grow, as each finds the defects in the other and, perhaps more painfully, in one's self. However, marriage is meant to make it easier, because of one's love, to surmount such defects. "Surmount" them—since remedy may not be possible. Many defects in any human being are permanent as long as this life lasts. It is, perhaps, especially hard for a husband to learn to rejoice in the woman that God has given him, not as meeting some abstract ideal of his own but as she is in herself, something far greater than any adolescent dream: a real human person destined for eternal life with God.

The symbolism of sexual intercourse also shows us why marriage is essentially monogamous, meant to link only one man to only one woman. That a woman should have but one husband seems symbolically clear. No matter how many men, one after another, she might choose to open herself to, if she conceives at all, unlikely enough in those circumstances, it is the sperm cell from but one of those many partners that is joined with the ovum of her body to initiate a new human life. She cannot multiply the gift of her substance according to the number of men who lie with her. Psychologically also, a woman, even if promiscuous, tends to dream of one man to whom she might eventually give herself.

It's a little different for the man. As we have mentioned, a man can have fertile intercourse with many women. He can beget a child on each of them. So, polygamy—one man as husband for several wives—does not have the wrongness of polyandry—one woman as wife for several husbands. In much of human history and in many societies, polygamy has been well established, God permitting it for a long while even in Israel.

Hence one might think that the full symbolism would be present in each case; yet this is not quite true. For although the husband can multiply his activity and the giving of his substance, the gift of himself to one woman means deprivation for another. There is division, not unity. Polygamy is, then, a highly defective kind of marriage. For, ideally, at least, in a man's relations to one wife, their children, their neighbors, and God, none of the things he gives to one need be taken from another. The reason is that these loves can all be well-ordered, one with respect to another. But the love that a man would have for several wives cannot be so ordered. He cannot give himself rightly to one without depriving another of the love she reasonably desires. Thus, monogamy is the proper form of even natural marriage, in the sense that it is the fullest, richest, that which most perfectly respects the symbolism of sexual union.

Natural marriage, then, is constituted by a reciprocal vow or promise—at least to each other, perhaps to God— to do all things with love, not merely the act of intercourse itself but everything signified by this act, that is, the totality of their life together. Consequently, it also involves the right to receive everything in love.

When we look at our lives, we see that much of what we do, whether with respect to God or to other people, comes not from love but from selfishness. Hence, marriage is a commitment to grow in selflessness. It is a commitment to a sort of asceticism, often also to penitence and reparation for the evil things we sometimes do to one another. So we are enabled to grow and progressively to bring our selfishness under control by learning to give ourselves in selfless love to each other; through each other, to our children; and so, to all men, all from an ever growing love for God.

Consequently, the act of intercourse is a symbol not merely of marriage in a static sense but of marriage as progress and as growth. For, we can only utter its full meaning when we have learned, through asceticism and through penance, the self-control that is needed to get beyond our selfishness. Only then can we truly mean and fully intend in mind and heart what our act of intercourse actually says in and through a symbolism that, strong as it is naturally, has been charged by God with even greater meaning through His revelation.

4

Sexual Symbolism in the Scriptures

SEXUALITY IN SCRIPTURE

Since we wish to gain from the Scripture an understanding of the meaning of our sexuality, especially in its relation to Christ, we should note first that Scripture speaks of sex in several ways.

There are many scriptural accounts of human sexual behavior, sometimes with comment, sometimes without. The Bible is forthright about such matters; and, although it does not emphasize sex, it does not hesitate to say what it means. We are told, for example, that David desired Bathsheba, had her brought to him, lay with her, made her pregnant, and had her husband murdered to prevent his discovering David's action. Such straightforward narratives about sexual activity, especially when, as in David's case, they are accompanied with God's judgment as to its wrongness or rightness, make clear to us some facts of a moral nature about sexual behavior. But they rarely do more than suggest the significance of sexual activity apart from those particular circumstances.

We learn much about God through knowledge of His Law, seeing what He has thought important to command or forbid us to do. From the commandment, "You shall not commit adultery," for example, we learn something of His concern for human fidelity in marriage. But, again, the reasons for the prohibition, its intrinsic meaning, and reasonableness are left in the dark. There are many, very detailed regulations concerning sexual matters in the books of the Law; and in the New Testament, St. Paul tosses off whole series of injunctions for Christian sexual behavior, refining the Old-Testament ones, omitting some, or adding others. But just such alterations raise serious questions as to whether or how far even his injunctions might be mutable as times change.

Yet, the Bible has vastly more to say about sex than is contained in its narratives or laws. Chiefly by use of sexual symbolism, it tells us of the meaning of sex and offers grounds for understanding sexual morality. No symbol contains, however, the fullness of the reality it points to. It is never possible to find in the symbol all that is, in fact, true of the mystery that is symbolized. Hence, we are not trying here to construct a *proof* from the symbolism. Rather, accepting the Church's Tradition, we seek to see how her teaching is consistent with and enlightened by this symbolism. This latter cannot be treated as an independent source whence one could force a position on the Church. The Scriptures are to be understood, as Catholics have always sought to understand them, in the way the Church that wrote and collected them, identified and transmitted them, has understood them. If someone says, then, that our use of symbolism here is not coercive as an argument, we must agree; it is not meant to be.

First of all, we need to distinguish two kinds of sexual symbols that are easily confused. The more common "sexual symbols" are those, so much studied today in psychological and psychiatric circles, that are symbols *of* sexuality. That is, something that is not sexual is used as a symbol of something that is.

For example, the rose, which is not sexual as people ordinarily perceive it, is taken as a symbol of a woman's sexuality. The snake, for equally obvious reasons, is in many cultures taken as a symbol for a man's sexuality. Evidently, one may use such sexual symbols to avoid explicit or even conscious reference to sexual matters. And conversely, a psychiatrist may learn a patient's unconscious attitudes towards repressed sexual events through observation of his use of such symbols.

There are many such symbols in the Bible, the rose and the snake among them. But our interest here is not primarily with these. While they may illustrate more deeply the nature of sexual activity itself and not merely, as some wrongly assume, rehearse surreptitiously its physical description, yet they cannot go beyond that to the meaning and significance of that activity.

But there is another meaning of "sexual symbols," that is, those that symbolize *by* or *through* sexuality. As seen in Chapter 3 above, sex organs, sexual emotions and psychic reactions, the marital act itself, or even an entire marriage are symbols of things other than themselves and beyond themselves, of spiritual things that are not sexual at all.

This is the sort of sexual symbolism that Scripture is richest in. God uses the natural symbolism of our sexual activity and relationships to tell us much about Himself and our relations with Him. How this is done is best seen by turning to the Scripture and discovering how God has in fact revealed to us the supernatural meaning of sex.

CHRIST AND HIS BRIDE

To begin at the beginning, we find in the second chapter of *Genesis* the story of the creation of Eve. In the Garden of Eden, God has just created man and is showing him the animals. "The man gave names to all cattle, and to the birds of the air, and to every beast of the field; but for the man there was not found a helper fit for him."

In the ancient Semitic world, a name indicated a being's innermost nature or destiny. To give something a name, then, or to change its name meant to be able to know its inner nature, to govern it accordingly, and to determine its destiny. Here, then, man is being set over the animals; God is giving him the power to govern and even change them, and to share the divine dominion over them. But none was found that could be a helpmate for man and be his companion. Man is master of creation but he is alone; for, nothing in creation is his equal. Then

> the LORD God caused a deep sleep to fall upon the man, and while he slept took one of his ribs and closed up its place with flesh; and the rib which the LORD God had taken from the man he made into a woman and brought her to the man.

God makes the woman from the man. Her being is drawn from his. Of the same species, they are equals. Though different, they are to be made one.

> Then the man said, "This at last is bone of my bones and flesh of my flesh; she shall be called Woman, because she was taken out of Man." Therefore a man leaves his father and his mother and cleaves to his wife and they become one flesh. And the man and his wife were both naked, and were not ashamed (*Genesis* 2:20-25).

This is the first mention in the Scriptures of a symbolic theme that will be often repeated till their very end: that the sexual union of man and woman makes them two in one single flesh. Here, the obvious sense of this theme is that the bodily union of man and woman in intercourse represents in some way and symbolizes the fullness of their psychological union as a couple and as parents, united not only in their own sexual union but in the flesh of their children.

In the time between this passage from *Genesis* and the great prophets who arose during the last years of the Divided Kingdom, the biblical teaching on the right use of one's sexual powers is set forth in great detail but always in purely secular terms.

For example, the sexual union of Abraham and Sarah, through which Isaac was conceived, is the first fulfillment of that promise which initiates the history of salvation. But their marriage, though approved and blessed by God, is not sacred except insofar as God protects it from infringement by the king of Egypt. Nor is their intercourse seen as a religious rite. Later, in the Law, there are many detailed prescriptions with regard to sexual behavior, prohibitions as well as things to be done. But there is no hint that there is anything sacred in any positive sense about what is sexual. On the other hand, even in marital union, any flow of seed seems to have made both partners ritually unclean.

The reason for this is that God Himself has no sexuality. God is not male, though He is infinitely masculine. In His own nature He is spirit, without sexuality, which as such belongs only to creatures and, so, lies wholly outside the domain of religion and the sacred. This awareness was one of the major gifts of divine revelation to man's religious life upon earth. Divine sexuality was always to be a sign of paganism and idolatry.

It must have come, then, as a great surprise to the Israelites when suddenly the prophet Hosea was inspired to speak of Israel's relation to God in terms of human sexual union.

Hosea is the first to develop, bluntly and straightforwardly, another theme which continues through the rest of Scripture. This is the theme of the people of Israel as the unfaithful bride of the LORD, the God of Israel. Hosea begins abruptly by saying, "The LORD said to Hosea, 'Go, take to yourself a wife of harlotry and have children of harlotry, for the land commits great harlotry by forsaking the LORD.'" What he is talking about is their worship of idols, of the gods of the peoples around them, and their seeking to live in accord with the standards of their more powerful and cultured neighbors.

God continues:

> Plead with your mother, plead—for she is not my wife, and I am not her husband—that she put away her harlotry from her face and her adultery from between her breasts; lest I strip her naked and make her as in the day she was born.

Then He threatens to take away from her everything He has given her. Notice the strong sexual symbolism He is using here, of a wife engaging in prostitution, opening herself to every comer. This symbol itself is sexual but it is chosen to illustrate something spiritual, to represent in human terms the horror of unfaithfulness to God. Sexual misconduct is included among the sins for which Israel is being rebuked, but only as one item among many. The great crime is that they have gone after idols; if they are unjust to the poor, are liars, thieves, adulterers, all this is just one or other way of denying the LORD's sovereignty by rejecting His commandments in the service of alien gods.

He continues:

> She shall pursue her lovers, but not overtake them; and she shall seek them, but shall not find them. Then she shall say, "I will go and return to my first husband, for it was better with me then than now."

This, of course, was forbidden by the Law. If a wife, divorced by her husband, married another, she could never return to the former husband. If he took her back, both became unclean. But the LORD is above His Law.

> Therefore, behold, I will allure her, and bring her into the wilderness, and speak tenderly to her ... And there she shall answer as in the days of her youth, as at the time when she came out of the land of Egypt. [And now speaking to Israel directly,] And in that day ... you will call me "My husband" ... And I will betroth you to me forever; I will betroth you to me in righteousness and in justice, in steadfast love, and in mercy. I will betroth you to me in faithfulness; and you shall know the LORD (*Hosea* 1:2, 2:2-20).

Clearly, the symbolism has gone well beyond that of an adulterous wife. For, God is taking back His unfaithful people to Himself, as a husband might take back a wife he loves in spite of her unfaithfulness. Infidelity to the LORD is to be understood only through this symbol of adultery, this rending of the most intimate of human bonds; and God's forgiveness, only through the outrageous violation of the Law by a love-smitten husband taking back the adulteress. God uses marital union and sexual infidelity to symbolize relations that completely transcend the sexual, His love and permanent fidelity towards His people, in spite even of their idolatry.

This theme is developed at length through the rest of the Old Testament and also the New. Ezekiel, to give but one example, tells us more about the original wedding, tells us how Israel had been begotten by a wandering Aramean of a Hittite mother, how (referring to Israel's being led out of Egypt and the long journey through the desert) the LORD had picked her up, washed her of her blood, let her grow up and then said:

> And you grew up and became tall and arrived at full maidenhood; your breasts were formed,

and your hair had grown; yet you were naked and bare. When I passed by you again and looked upon you, behold, you were at the age for love; and I spread my skirt over you, and covered your nakedness; yea, I plighted my troth to you and entered into a covenant with you ... and you became mine. Then I bathed you with water and washed off your blood from you, and anointed you with oil. I clothed you also with embroidered cloth and shod you with leather, I swathed you in fine linen and covered you with silk. And I decked you with ornaments, and put bracelets on your arms, and a chain on your neck. And I put a ring on your nose, and earrings in your ears, and a beautiful crown upon your head (*Ezekiel* 16:6-14).

Thus, the LORD recalls His wedding with Israel, His dearly beloved, His bride, although she had since proven so often adulterous and had fornicated so often with idols and alien gods.

The final Old-Testament presentation of this attitude of God to His people and, in some ways, the strongest is found in *The Song of Songs*, a book which sometimes has given offense to Christians. It is filled with glowing, incandescent love-poetry, sensuous and rich, strongly sexual in its imagery. There is no mistaking its natural meaning.

Yet, in another sense, there has been a great mistake as to its meaning. Many people see nothing in it beyond its sensuality. But Jewish and Christian traditions have agreed in seeing that this love-poetry, whatever its original sources, was being interpreted by the author as God's love-song for His people and theirs for Him, as His rejoicing in His bride and her rejoicing in Him. It is the bright reflection into the present of a future in which God and Israel will be made perfectly one with each other—Israel no longer unfaithful, seeking only the LORD even when He seems to have vanished and she cannot find Him, not turning aside after anyone else.

The impact of all this on Israel was very deep. The fidelity of the LORD to His one bride despite her faults and infidelities began to make clear to His people the ideal of human marriage, that this too could only be monogamous, one husband with one wife. The perfection of monogamy, which would also ban remarriage after divorce, was to come only with the Messiah, our Lord Jesus, who alone could give to His Church the fullness of grace which this ideal would require. Yet ordinary polygamy did wither away in the Judaism of the last centuries before Christ as God's people began to understand more fully this symbol of God's love.

Some people may say, "Well, that's fine for the Old Testament. The Jews were a carnal people." One difficulty with this reaction is that one finds as much sexual symbolism in the New Testament, though the image is changed slightly. Instead of Israel's being described as the bride of the LORD, it is the Church, the New Israel, that is presented as the bride of Christ.

In the Gospels, our Lord makes frequent use of the traditional sexual imagery of the Old Testament. Thus, He often speaks of "an adulterous generation," a phrase that has become so commonplace that we hardly any longer advert to its meaning. What He means by it is precisely what the prophets meant, that His generation of Jews were in fact committing adultery, though this time not with idols. Their refusal to accept Christ, their refusal to see in Him at least a prophet sent by God, showed that Israel's heart was fixed elsewhere and, consequently, was adulterous. She was once again faithless.

Further, Jesus uses nuptial imagery often in speaking of the kingdom of heaven. "The kingdom of heaven may be compared to a king who made a wedding feast for his son ...," where of course the king is God the Father and His Son is our Lord. Or, again, the kingdom is like ten virgins waiting for the bridegroom to return from the wedding feast to take his bride into his house.

Even John the Baptist, that rugged ascetic out in the desert, subsisting on grasshoppers and wild honey, clothed in rough camel's hair, refers to Christ in just such terms. When John's disciples indignantly asked how it was that Jesus also was baptizing and drawing people away from John, he replied,

> You yourselves bear me witness, that I said, "I am not the Christ, but I have been sent before Him. He who has the bride is the bridegroom; the friend of the bridegroom, who stands and hears him, rejoices greatly at the bridegroom's voice; therefore this joy of mine is now full. He must increase, but I must decrease (*John* 3:28-30).

He is referring to Christ our Lord as the bridegroom of Israel and of all His Church.

St. Paul takes up the same theme in several places. Most important for our purposes is the passage in *Ephesians*, where he instructs us that husbands are to love their wives

> as Christ loved the Church and gave Himself up for her, that He might sanctify her, having cleansed her by the washing of water with the word [referring to baptism on the one hand and to the Jewish prenuptial bath on the other] that He might present the Church to Himself in splendor, without spot or wrinkle or any such thing, that she might be holy and without blemish. Even so, husbands should love their wives as their own bodies. He who loves his wife loves himself. For no man ever hates his own flesh, but nourishes and cherishes it, as Christ does the Church, because we are members of His body. [Now, referring back to *Genesis*] "For this reason a man shall leave his

father and mother and be joined to his wife and the two shall become one flesh.'' This is a great mystery, and I mean in reference to Christ and the Church (*Ephesians* 5:22-33).

Notice here he has mixed two metaphors, two images of the Church. The Church is the bride of Christ; as members of the Church, therefore, we are made members of His body because He is one flesh with her.

St. Paul uses this same theme in exhorting his Corinthians against fornication.

Do you not know that he who joins himself to a prostitute becomes one body with her? For, as it is written, "The two shall become one flesh." But he who is united to the Lord becomes one spirit with Him (*1 Corinthians* 6:15-17).

The union of Christ with His Church, then, affects each of us individually. Since a man's sexual union with a woman, even in fornication, makes the two of them one flesh, the Christian may not fornicate because to do so would be to join Christ's body, whose member he is, to the body of a whore. So strongly does St. Paul see the one union to be the symbol of the other!

This imagery is brought to its fullness when we come to *Revelation*, (*Apocalypse*), where we find that even our final union with God in heaven is described in the same way.

"Hallelujah! For the Lord our God the Almighty reigns. Let us rejoice and exult and give Him the glory, for the marriage of the Lamb [that is, the Lamb of God, the Lamb standing as slain forever] has come and His Bride has made herself ready; it was granted her to be clothed with fine linen, bright and pure"—for the fine linen is the righteous deeds of the saints .... "Blessed are those who are invited to the marriage supper of the Lamb."

And in describing the consummation of all things, he says

> Then I saw a new heaven and a new earth; for
> the first heaven and the first earth had passed
> away, and the sea was no more. And I saw the
> holy city, new Jerusalem, coming down out of
> heaven from God, prepared as a bride adorned
> for her husband (*Revelation* 19:6-9, 21:1-2).

Heaven, to which all of us look forward, the consummation of the world, is shown to us as the wedding, the marriage-feast of Christ to and with His Church, the consummation of that union in eternity.

FATHER, MOTHER, AND CHILDREN

If we look carefully at the scriptural passages that deal with the spousal relations between God and His people or between Christ and His Church, we find that most of them say nothing at all about children, even when, as in *Eph.* 5:22-33, for example, children are talked about in the verses immediately following. Further, where children *are* mentioned, they are not begotten of that spousal relationship.

This strange omission of children from the sexual symbolism we have seen in the Bible so far is balanced, however, by two other scriptural symbolisms: maternity and adoptive paternity.

From at least the time of the prophet Hosea, the Old Testament speaks of God as Father, as the One who has brought Israel to be. A few examples will suffice.

Hosea writes: "When Israel was a child, I [the LORD] loved him, and out of Egypt I called my son ... it was I who taught Ephraim to walk," (11:1-4). In *Isaiah* we find, "The LORD has spoken: 'Sons have I reared and brought up ....' Ah, sinful nation, offspring of evildoers, sons who deal corruptly!" (1:2,4). Note how, within three verses He speaks of the people of Judah as sons He has reared and yet as the sinful offspring of evildoers. Already, we can see that God's children are His by adoption. Their natural birth as human individuals is attributed to their human parents; God is not called their Father because of creation.

In *Deuteronomy*, Moses says of Israel,

> "They are no longer His children because of their blemish ... Is He not your father, who created you, who made you and established you? ... Ask your father and he will show you ..." [Again, God's fatherhood is not that of their natural fathers. Though creation of each person in the womb may be a factor in His fatherhood, this is more likely a reference to His creating them His own people.] "You were unmindful of the Rock that bore you and you forgot the God who gave you birth. The LORD saw it and spurned them, because of the provocation of His sons and daughters. And He said, 'I will hide my face from them ... for they are ... children in whom is no faithfulness'" (32:5,6,7,18-20).

Much later, Second Isaiah prays to the LORD, "For You are our Father, though Abraham does not know us ... You, O LORD, are our Father" (*Is.* 63:16; cf.64:8).

Only in *Ezekiel* does one find a link between the symbolism of fatherhood and that of husband and wife. Even this is indirect, by way of the symbolism of the motherhood of Jerusalem. Thus, the LORD says, "You took your sons and your daughters, whom you had borne to me, and these you sacrificed to them [idols] to be devoured ... you slaughtered my children" (*Ez.* 16:20-21). There is a similar language again in *Ez.* 23:4,37.

The notion that His people bears children for God, then, though visible in the Old Testament, is much muted. There is, however, even in these passages of *Ezekiel*, no direct begetting by God of the children of His spouse. The basic relationship, though the word is not used, is that of adoption. Born naturally of human parents, they are made His when He espouses Jerusalem, their mother. She has borne them for Him, but not by Him.

With the coming of our Lord, there is a sudden clarity of focus. The same sexual symbolisms recur. But now the relationships become much more complex, for God is revealed to be not only Father but Son and Holy Spirit, only one Being yet three distinct Persons.

There is only one Father, from whom not only every family and lineage but every fatherhood and all those called father (*Mt.* 23:9) take their name. There is only one natural begetting by Him, the eternal generation of His eternal Son and Word, Jesus Christ (e.g., *Jn.* 1:1-5,18).

We are made children of the Father by being made the brothers of Jesus, not as if the Father begot other sons than Jesus, but by being given a share in the life of Jesus (*Gal.* 3:26-27). Thus, with the sole exception of Jesus, His Only-Begotten, all the children of God are *adopted* (e.g., *Gal.* 4:5; *Rom.* 8:23,29-30).

This adoption, however, unlike all human adoption, gives a new principle of life, the Holy Spirit. (Hence, in the *First Letter of John* especially, John speaks of our adoption as our being born or begotten of God, a phrase he never applies to our Lord.) The Holy Spirit is the Spirit of the Father, who has given Him to Jesus triumphant—for He is also the Spirit of the Son—to give to us. The Spirit, then, as Spirit of Jesus, cries out "Abba! Father!" within our hearts as He did in Christ's Heart (*Rom.* 8:13-17). It is the Spirit who makes us sons of God, by making us one with Christ, the only Son (Cf. *Jn.* 3:3-8). The reality here lies painfully far beyond and above all symbols; but they can still give us endless light if we use them as the Church would have us do.

But there is another symbolism needed here, for to God's adoptive fatherhood the Bible adds the corresponding motherhood of the Church. As in the Old Testament, our adoption takes place in principle when God takes His people as His bride. This was done, once for all, when He died for her on the cross (*Eph.* 5:25-27).

But Christ is nowhere said to beget children of His Church: He is the Son, not Father of anyone. He enters into no sexual union with His bride. (This, it is important to understand, does no damage to the spousal symbolism. The sexual union between husband and wife is, indeed, the best symbol we have for the quality of love between Christ and His Church. Yet Christ's love for the Church is not sexual, though a man's love for his wife, which is sexual, can be more like Christ's love for the Church than any other natural love a man may have.)

The question then is: How do we become her children if the Son does not generate children of the Church for the Father? For, she is without spot or wrinkle, and we are born into this world outside of her and in sin. Natural birth does not suffice, as it did among the Israelites, to make us members of His people.

As just seen, Christ's union with her leaves her still a virgin. The ancient tradition of the Church has, therefore, compared her to Mary. She brings forth virginally, as Mary did, the members of Christ's Body. Just as the Holy Spirit was the agent of the Father's begetting of the human nature of the Son of the virginal Mary, so He is the agent of the Father's regenerating us of the virginal Church into the life of Christ. Thus, we can be truly said to be born of the Spirit (*Jn.* 3:9).

In sum, we find, from the first page of the Scriptures to the last, the varied aspects of man's sexual life being used to symbolize the relationships between God and His people. Man's vocation and dignity, his sins, his redemption, and final glorification are presented to us under the imagery of birth, marriage, infidelity, penitence, a renewal of vows and a final reunion, which becomes perfect union in eternity. This symbolism all of us must understand, for it shows us what God thinks of our sexuality: something so greatly good that it can be used to express the deepest and the highest truths about the relations between God and man.

5

The Church:
Bride of Christ and
Mother of the Living

We have seen how natural marriage is the institutional expression of the natural meaning of sexual intercourse. In the sacrament of matrimony, Christ takes up this natural marriage to symbolize something far beyond it. Even as intercourse symbolizes marriage, as bodily union signifies an entire life together, so God has made natural marriage to symbolize something that lies entirely beyond the sexual: the relations between Christ and His Church, and the Father's adopting us as His children through Christ's gift of the Spirit to His bride. God has made marriage to symbolize relationships more intimate than its own sexual relationship, stronger, more tender, more open, more demanding. This sacramental symbolism involves all that is present in the marital relationship but gives it a further meaning at a level of communion where there is no possibility, even, of sexual activity.

CHRIST'S UNMERITED LOVE FOR HIS CHURCH

Christ's love was not given to the Church for any merit on her own part. The Father freely chose this people as His Son's bride; and Christ loves her because she is the Father's choice for Him. He had to win her for Himself by His battle with Satan upon the cross. He espoused her there when His side was pierced, His Heart was opened, and water flowed forth, the sign of the bridal bath of baptism. He had not found her worthy of Himself; only His death made her to be a bride without spot or wrinkle or any such thing. Her beauty was His gift alone.

As a husband with his wife, it is Christ who is the initiator of union with His Church. As God is masculine with respect to the whole of His creation and with respect to the whole of humanity, Christ is masculine with regards to His Church. The Church has no initiative in relation to Christ except that which Christ has already given to her. Without His grace, she can do nothing.

Christ takes pleasure in His Church as a husband takes pleasure in his bride. Finding His delight in her, He seeks to share with her all His gifts. Since He experiences the Church's happiness as His own, He gives to her everything that He has to offer to mankind. Only through her, though often in ways that are not visible to us, do His gifts reach the world of men. Those who have somewhat scornfully pinned the tag "triumphalism" on her claim that Christ has loved her this much show merely that they do not share very strongly His love for her.

Chief of His gifts is the Holy Spirit. Through the Spirit, He guards the Church from harm and keeps her faithful to Himself. By the power of His Spirit, He maintains her in purity of doctrine and worship. By the Spirit's action, the Church conceives and bears children for the Father. Since through the Spirit we live with Christ's own life, we are nurtured and brought to spiritual maturity under her guidance and love.

The Church, on the other hand, must be receptive of grace and has to respond to the love Christ has shown her. She may not be simply passive. If one needs any argument against a woman's being passive in marriage, one would find it right here. For, that which she symbolizes through her part in the marital act is the Church's response to Christ. Passivity as her "response" would destroy this symbolism. (The one exception would occur when, by her husband's engaging in something evil, the act has already been so changed in what it symbolizes that any active response by her would signify cooperation in evil.)

The Church responds to Christ to give Him pleasure, having her sole pleasure in Him and in the fact that He takes pleasure in her response. From this, we can see that the Church's interest in seeking new members is not simply fear that those who are not visibly hers will be lost.

Not only Christians today, after Vatican II, but the Old Testament and the Church Fathers knew that God had revealed Himself beyond the limits of Israel, as He did, for example, to the Pharaohs known by Abraham and by Joseph, to Balaam, and to the "Babylonian kings" of *Daniel.* They knew that God gives to every man the grace to be saved, even though he has not heard of Christ from other men.

Neither, however, does the Church so disesteem her Lord's fidelity as to think that all have access to Him and to salvation if not, somehow, through her. Her apostolate has an urgency that implies much more than bringing mere academic knowledge of Christ to others, or theological theories about Him.

If the Church is so concerned to bring ever more people to the knowledge of Christ, it is that she may bring forth for the Father through His Spirit all those whom Christ desires as His brothers. There is no race, there are no cultures, there are no tribes or languages which are naturally alien to her. All are meant to be within her; all are meant to be her children. As the Fathers of the Church said repeatedly, "He alone has God as Father who first has the Church as mother."

CHRIST'S FIDELITY TO HIS CHURCH

As seen in Chapter 3, sexual intercourse symbolizes the fidelity that is institutionalized in natural marriage. In the sacrament of matrimony, this natural fidelity is made to symbolize the fidelity of God Himself. Christ's union with His Church is wholly incapable of dissolution. There is no way it can be undone in time or in eternity. For, Christ cannot be faithless. He is always faithful even when we are unfaithful. He cannot go back on His covenant with His Church, no matter how faithless the Church may seem to be in the eyes of the world because of the sins of her children. He knew that we would not be fully faithful, and He died to deliver us from the evils of our unfaithful hearts.

At this point one might object and argue that divorce with remarriage is indeed possible, for the Lord has changed wives Himself. He was first wedded to Israel, but has now abandoned her. Because she was unfaithful and rejected Him, He has divorced her and married the Church of the Gentiles.

But, He has not abandoned Israel. St. Paul tells us that Israel is an olive tree from which the branches have been broken off through their own fault. We, the branches of wild olive trees, were incapable of bearing any fruit except what is bitter and hard, of no use at all. But through our being made one with Christ, we have been grafted into the still-standing trunk of Israel, the trunk of the patriarchs, prophets, and kings. Thus we have been enabled to bear fruit that is sweet and good.

We, by being incorporated into Christ, are the new Israel, but only in the sense that we are made one with the old, being new growth from the same roots and trunk. The branches that have been broken off are no longer drawing life from the trunk of Israel, though still calling themselves by that name. But God in His fidelity wishes to bring them back and graft them in again. For, just as a branch broken from a tree can still live with what remains in it of the life of the tree and even after a time can still be saved if it is grafted back in, so, St. Paul tells us, God will graft back these branches.

There remains, then, only the one true people of God. The Church is not a new bride. We now see that she has indeed to be described less statically than she herself once thought, when her only children had but one lineage. The changes brought by her growth and maturation have been more surprising and disconcerting than those changes a girl undergoes at puberty. But they are the same sort of changes: those she has needed to become ready to bear children. So, the Church is Israel grown up, become mature, and bearing children for the Father from among the Gentiles.

And when Israel according to the flesh reaches her supernatural maturity, when those who are Jews by carnal generation finally recognize their Lord and come to Him, then all the promises to Israel will be fulfilled. This will also be the fulfillment of all that He has given to the Gentiles. It will be, St. Paul says, "life from the dead," the consummation and perfection of the Church, when His bride will be radiant in the beauty of all her children as well as in herself.

The fundamental limitations on bodily union in sexual relations symbolize, we have seen, reverence and awe for one's partner, who has been created for God and is owned by Him alone. Such reverence signifies in its turn Christ's reverence and respect for the freedom of His Church. He permits the Church to go her own way—here we are speaking of the local churches, for the Church Universal, like Mary, is indefectible by God's special favor, though always free. The local church will suffer for her sins. She will go into exile from those regions where she is unfaithful. Always, however, there is the promise that, as with ancient Israel, if she returns, He will forgive. The words of the prophets remain true for the new Israel as well as for the old.

OUR SEXUALITY IN THE LIGHT OF CHRIST'S MYSTERIES

All these things apply to each of us individually as members of the Church. As we come to understand these mysteries somewhat, we will find that they teach us much more than we have yet understood about our own sexuality. The supernatural perfection that is symbolized by marital union will reflect its splendor back upon our own sexual activity and make us see things not visible except to those who know by faith its ultimate meaning.

Only in this context does Christ's teaching against divorce-with-remarriage make sense. Sacramental marriage is not just the union of man and woman, still weak in love, seeking to sustain and help one another. Nor is it, as often thought, a mere contract between the two parties. Christian marriage is part of a solemn covenant, not so much with each other as with Christ.

For, Christ's espousal of His bride upon the cross was the sealing of the New Covenant in His blood. The children of this covenant enter into it, then, and ratify it in their own persons by their marriage, as they image forth and symbolically represent Christ's marriage to His Church. This is the ultimate reason why husband and wife are called to sacrifice themselves, as far as death if need be, for the true good of one another. For, our Lord commanded us, "Love one another as I have loved you"; and the way He loved us was to sacrifice Himself for the unfaithful upon the cross. As each Mass renews this sacrifice and as each Communion strengthens Christ's union with His bride, so Christian marriage is the sacramental representation of the covenant of eternal love Christ has entered into with His Church.

Thus, Christ's own fidelity is engaged to enable husband and wife always to be faithful. If they will genuinely rely on this covenant that God has made with them through His Son, lean on His promise, trust that fidelity which is eternal and immutable, no matter what the circumstances, then their fidelity is assured as they transcend their own weaknesses in Him. His Spirit, whom St. Paul calls the "down payment," the "deposit," the "pledge," is given already as the bond of their espousal.

Corresponding to the giving of one person to the other through the gift of a man's substance to his wife, we have God's gift of Himself to us through His Holy Spirit, who pours out the love of the Father in our hearts and who makes us sharers in the life of Christ by grace. We give ourselves to the Father, in turn, through the same Spirit, by responding to His grace actively even as a woman opens herself to her husband in love.

So, all of us, whatever our walk of life, when we seek to find the will of Christ for us, it is to give Him the pleasure of our serving Him as we should, of doing the things for Him that will give Him pleasure; and we find joy in that. "In His will is our peace."

As Christ has the sole initiative in relation to His Church, so there is nothing that we can do to initiate any process with regards to God or with regards to our Lord. It is Catholic doctrine, solemnly defined as far back as the sixth century, that we cannot desire any grace unless God has already given us His grace to desire it, that we cannot in any way long to repent or seek sorrow for our sins unless God has already given us the grace to do so. He alone can take the initiative; only He can convert us.

In fact, He need not wait upon our willingness. If He does not take the initiative, we will be unwilling and firmly set against any conversion. But His grace can still reach us and open us up and make it possible for us to be converted. Sooner or later, He does require our response, our cooperation; but the initiative is solely and exclusively His.

This doctrine gives us further proof of His love. By it we are taught that all our longings for His joy and peace and all our desires to know and love Him better and to serve Him more faithfully are signs of His love already at work. The mere presence of holy desires indicates an initiative that He has already taken. And, yet, Christ's love is like the love of a husband for his wife in this also, that it is a free love. The husband's love, unless it is no more than passion, results from a decision. He need not have offered it in the first place, though he has obligated himself now to love, in spite of all, because he freely promised to do so. So, Christ has done for us.

Knowing that they only procreate their children, good parents do not act as if they own them. They respect their freedom, according to their age and education, despite the pain that this respect for their freedom may cause them when the time comes for them to leave their parents' home to found their own. This parental respect symbolizes in its turn God's respect for our freedom and for us as persons. Although He could, God does not coerce the human will. At the moment of our death He will say to each of us, "Now, let your will be done!" And if our will then is to refuse Him our love and service and to insist upon our own ways rather than His, those will be the most terrible words a human heart can hear. Though He died in torment to prevent it, He will let us have our choice.

The symbolism of Christian marriage reaches even as far as the Beatific Vision—that absolute and perfect union of man with God that constitutes our utter happiness—that Scripture describes as the wedding feast of the Lamb and the final consummation of His marriage with His Church. The Church will then be united with her Spouse in a spiritual ecstasy far beyond all marital ecstasy as she enters the joy of her Lord. As St. Paul says, "God will be all in all." God, on His part, will rejoice totally in His creatures now made perfect, now fully His, now at last what He intended them to be from the beginning, in every way in His image, Jesus our Lord, and according to the Likeness which is His Spirit.

But far beyond all created things, there is the life of the Trinity Itself, the eternal giving of the three Persons to one another. The Father gives the totality of the divine nature to the Son, giving Him everything that He, the Father, has except simply His being Father. The Father through the Son gives the totality of the nature that they possess in common to the Holy Spirit, who receives actively Their gift so as to be one being with Them, except for that which constitutes Them Father or Son. It is this life of total gift and of total response, that is the ultimate thing symbolized by the act of sexual intercourse. This is its tremendous sacredness, its tremendous intrinsic holiness.

With this background, we can now understand the basic principle of Christian sexual morality: We ought so to engage in the natural sexual activity of body, mind, and heart that its basic symbolic structure is always preserved and honored, so that this structure may serve rightly to symbolize in turn the relations, in the Spirit of the Father, between Christ and His Church. If God has created marital union to signify these great mysteries of the faith, how great a responsibility, then, lies on married couples (and, in their own way, on all the unmarried) so to act that this meaning and significance is fully preserved in their action and is meant and intended by them!

This principle contains within itself, I think, the full range of all Catholic sexual morality. It explains, too, why the Church has held the positions she has held in all those varying domains where people had thought her inconsistent, holding one thing as to one type of human sexual behavior and something else as to another. No, if understood from this point of view, all her teaching falls in place as simple and consistent. Christ is the norm. His relations to His Father and to His bride the Church form the norms for union among Christians in their marriages and families. Indeed, as possibly suggested already by the examples we have considered, those relations are norms for all sexual behavior whatever.

6

Christ on the Cross: Sexual Lies and Counterfeits

We have spoken of the symbolism of sexual intercourse, of both its natural meaning and the meaning it has in the order of grace and redemption. We have seen that intercourse expresses its full meaning only in marriage and that marriage is the institution which crystallizes the intent, the purpose, the resolve of the two parties to discover together and to express fully to each other the integral meaning of this act.

But more than marriage is explained by the symbolism of sexual activity. The entire range of moral problems that all people confront in this domain can receive here a unified and straightforward explanation. We will consider first what makes certain sexual actions wrong even at the natural level; then we will look at each again from the point of view of God's revelation.

NATURAL SYMBOLISM OF MISUSE OF SEX

On the natural level, what God asks of us is that we truly "do what comes naturally." This is not a matter of mere spontaneous liking and desire, but of what is in accordance with the nature He has given us. For, our nature is a share in His, even apart from the life of grace, since our nature and entire being is made according to the Image of God which is Christ.

At this level, we can restate the principle mentioned at the end of the preceding chapter: We may never use sexual activity, the living and naturally symbolic language of marital love, to tell a lie; nor may we ever corrupt it by using our sexual powers and organs for actions that are only seemingly sexual, but whose meaning has been radically altered.

Lies

The first type of abuse of the sexual powers, then, is falsehood. The "word" one says is integral; the symbol is undamaged. One's sexual activity is in full conformity on the physical level with the way such actions should be done. One says, "I love you" with his body, but his mind is saying something else. The genuine "word" of love is used to tell a lie.

Consider adultery, for example. The man and the woman committing the adultery are having intercourse, usually lovingly and in such a way that no one could tell from watching them that they are not married. But though they are saying in the symbolic language of the body, "I am wholly yours, yours alone, forever," at least one of them knows that this is not true. At least one cannot give himself to the other since he already belongs to someone else. At least one is wrenching apart his bond of commitment to his own wife or husband and attempting to confer the gift of self upon this other party. It is a lie, and a great lie, a falsehood that is able on the natural level to undercut a marriage and destroy it.

Usually less grave, but an all-too-common sin of falsehood within marriage itself, is the act of intercourse done without charity. This is most obvious when a husband forces sex upon his wife against her will. So doing, he makes the symbol of love serve for coercion, whereas true love reveres freedom; for personal satisfaction only, whereas love is for another; or for contempt or even hatred, the antitheses of love.

But a man can fail in charity also if he is inattentive to his wife's needs and pleasure during intercourse. Perhaps a minute after obtaining his own satisfaction, without regard to hers, he is snoring. On the other hand, a wife sins against charity who deliberately chooses to be cold, even frigid, towards her husband or who, without grave reason, refuses to cooperate with him. In such cases there is a withholding of the love that is symbolized by their actions; there is a rejection, in one way or another, of the personal element in the symbol; one is taking for oneself rather than giving to the other. What they mean by their act of intercourse is not what that intercourse means of itself.

Today, there is a widespread abuse grounded on the state's claim to grant a true divorce, i.e., to dissolve a genuine and valid marriage so completely that the former spouses are free henceforth to enter into new and valid marriages with new partners. But, in fact, whatever power the state may have over the marriages of the unbaptized, it has no power whatever to dissolve a Christian marriage. What really happens in most cases is that those who have pledged themselves permanently to each other to overcome all their defects of love reject this pledge and seek to break the covenant because of these very defects that they have solemnly undertaken to overcome together. Hence, their pledge to their new partners is a lie, since its sole basis is their refusal to honor such pledges. Their act of intercourse has become an adultery.

A different falsehood enters into the sin of fornication, i.e., when two people, as yet unmarried even though perhaps engaged, have intercourse with each other. They sin because they are saying by their act, "I am yours totally, irrevocably, forever," and yet in fact they know that, though they love each other, their gift is transient, that it is not complete. They know that they do not mean by this word of love what it means in itself. If they did mean it, they would be married, right on the spot, by common-law marriage; and they know that such is not their intention— or, if their intention, not within their power.

There is, of course, fornication that falls many moral levels below that between two people who love one another, even if not as much as they think they do. Promiscuity, bedding down with one "lover" after another, picking up somebody at a party or on the street, prostitution, etc., these things are far removed from truly human relationships. Indicating, at root, one's own selfishness and a contempt for other persons, such barefaced lies exclude from the sexual act almost everything God intended to be there except, at best, mere physical pleasure.

These actions spring from a sort of adolescent insecurity in the person that makes him seek out whatever prop he can find with which to bolster himself against this insecurity and to substitute for the adult person he feels lacking within himself. Having no sense of true personal identity, lacking "faces" in their own perception, such people engage in what might be called a faceless intercourse, often literally such. They are not interested enough in others as persons to want to see their faces; they dread being seen themselves as persons by another. Hence flow all the means used by profligates to keep their intercourse from becoming too personal.

The Substitute Symbol

On the other hand, there are abuses of the sexual powers which so alter the basic structures of sexual activity that the resultant actions have new and quite different meanings. The very nature of the act of intercourse is changed. Some fraud, some forgery, some shoddy substitute is passed off in place of the splendor of the integral act.

These altered acts are not necessarily lies; that is, the person who performs such an act need not mean something different from what that action means in itself. What is said by the altered symbol may be in fact a true statement made by the person using it; his mind and heart may be in accord with what he does sexually, though this need not be the case. But what he is saying is, itself, whether so intended or not, corrupt and evil because he has perverted and undone the nature of the sexual act. If the perfection of human nature is genuine and unflawed love, then acts that corrupt the bodily signs of such love are evil. Whether or not they are also used for telling lies, they symbolize some corruption of love or some refusal of love.

Consider the evil of masturbation. Though not a symbol of love at all, it is a symbol nonetheless: of withdrawal from reality, of self-pitying loneliness, of the sterility of the self loved in itself. What was meant for fertility, children, and family, the root and source of life and human community, is turned into a mechanism for pleasure, relief of tension, or material to use in a laboratory-analysis or a sperm-bank. Hence, masturbation is a symbol of fear and anxiety—of fear to love, of anxiety with regard to other people, withdrawing from them and seeking to live without them. Evidently, it symbolizes frustration. For there is no person to receive the power that is in the man's wasted seed; the woman's stimulation and orgasm result in nothing beyond themselves. Masturbation binds the person doing it to no one, but states symbolically personal ineffectiveness. One desires to avoid the risk of love and the responsibility of fruitfulness; he wishes to be by himself or, more tragically, passionately desires to love and to be loved yet chooses to be alone.

It is obvious, therefore, why masturbation can quickly become a habit. The person who performs such an act knows at least subconsciously what it symbolizes. He feels as a result deep shame, degradation, or inadequacy. These feelings increase his isolation and frustration and generate still stronger pressure to state in action his desperation, even without pleasure. One sin begets another.

Masturbation, then, poisons human happiness. It is almost impossible for anyone enslaved to such a habit to enter into marriage positively and fruitfully because masturbation chops away, at their roots, the love, the outgoingness, the generosity, the openness to life and to responsibility that the true sexual act is meant to have.

To cure a habit of this sort requires a real effort, under the competent direction, encouragement, and skillful advice of one's confessor. For, the problem is usually not principally a question of chastity or sexual purity. Masturbation is linked to everything in a person, to the entire personality and emotions; all aspects of one's life are in some way tied in to that act. It is the whole person, himself or herself, that is somehow frustrated, anxious, unwilling to love. But the rewards for making the effort are great. As this slavery is overcome, one becomes master of oneself and can grow at last to adulthood.

The symbolic structure of homosexual activity is similarly corrupt. What is ostensibly a symbol of love between two men or two women contains nothing that can truly be received, personally and as abiding gift, by the other person. It is a shallow symbol: of sentimentality, of perpetual juvenility and adolescent ambiguity, of not really knowing which sex one is, and of a sense of sexual inadequacy. Hence, those who so act will, typically, try to get closer to those of their own sex in order to discover and find themselves in these others rather than in their own selves. Or a man will seek weakly to draw or extract from others what he senses he lacks, rather than to acknowledge his responsibility for accepting its presence, already within him at least in germ, and so to grow to his own proper maturity.

Far more profoundly, there is no gift of one's substance for fruitfulness, no openness to the creation of human life. Each remains essentially alone. There is no true entry into the other as person, no lasting gift of one's self to the other, no genuine receptivity. All remains on the surface; each is the same after the act as before. Since in homosexual activity there cannot be true face-to-face communication, true intercourse, one with the other, is precluded. How far all this is from the total gift of one person to another in marriage is evident.

Homosexual activity involves, if not a radical contempt for one's own sex, for all sex in fact, then at least a fear of sexuality as such. For, sexuality implies another whose appeal is in that otherness and who is very different from oneself in body and temper of mind. But the person who is homosexually active fears the very nature of sexuality as something open to such difference. Often enough, this fear is accompanied by a certain hatred of the opposite sex. What is other is not needed, is declared not desirable; only what is like one's self fascinates and is sought in the other.

The solution to a problem of this sort, as is the case for any type of perversion, requires the effort of the whole person, because it is the whole person who is sick, not just his sexual appetite. In fact, the primary illness is not one of sexual desire at all. No matter what one's sexual attractions may be, whatever one's temptations are, if he is still capable of free choice, he is capable of chastity if he is humble enough to want and seek God's grace. The great illness here is self-pity and the consequent refusal to accept one's psychic condition as a call to at least temporary and total continence. But homosexual attractions, as such, need not make life intolerable. With God's help, they can be sanctifying, if only one sets about quietly to follow the commandments He has written into our nature.

One can now understand why the Church has always been so strongly opposed to contraception. Whatever its mode or variety, it substitutes something alien for the symbol of love. Contraceptives are either physical barriers or chemical withholdings of the conditions for fertility.

They enable what appears to be the marital act to be so performed that it now embodies an exclusion, a withholding, a negation of the most basic effect of sexual power. In the case of the woman, she refuses the power of the man over her body. In the case of the man, he refuses to let her fruitfulness present him with another like himself, whom he does not want.

In either case, what the barrier to sexual power or its withholding symbolically expresses is sterilization of one's partner or oneself. It is not, then, by accident that many who have accepted contraception sense no difference save in efficacy or convenience between condoms or diaphragms and the pill or IUD, or that many have now gone so far as to have themselves or their spouses permanently sterilized. The true symbol of love, mutual gift and reception is, in any case, excluded. Intercourse becomes the symbol of feminine dominance instead of masculine, of masculine impotence instead of strength.

Though it is possible that a couple intend what the contraceptive act says, I think that most, especially these days when even priests teach in contradiction to the Church, do not. There may well be true love between them, and no desire to set up barriers to love. Yet the psychological and moral power of this barricaded and obstructed union works gradually, slowly, imperceptibly, because of its intrinsic meaning and symbolic significance, on their subconscious and eventually on their conscious minds to generate that cold and self-centered hostility to new life known as the "contraceptive mentality."

More generally, the fact that one lies against the symbol of love or perverts it need not mean that there is no love present for the other party involved. There may well be deep love, but it is a love that is somehow disjointed. Hence come the terrible weight upon the conscience and the dull aching of heart that are the spiritual results of twisting the body's actions out of joint from their true meaning.

In sum, then, sexual symbols must only be used in

truth. If one cannot use them to express the truth, they should not be used at all. Further, no sexual symbol should be set aside to have something else substituted for it. If it is sometimes difficult to wait until one can use sexual action properly, the difficulty can always be overcome by steady reflection and prayer upon the true meaning and depth of love God has intended it to convey.

Natural family planning (NFP), we might mention in passing, is symbolically quite different. The couple knows, indeed, that they are not fertile as a couple, that he will not beget, she will not conceive. Yet the act itself is not altered. The couple remains essentially open to life; if not, there are easier means at hand they could be using.

It is perfectly true that the use of NFP can be selfish. A couple using NFP can mutually lock themselves in against children as effectively as they can with contraception. Yet this need not be the case; and the method itself helps against such misuse. For since one is not always free to have intercourse when using NFP, one is thereby invited to offer a greater gift, sacrificial in character, and to transcend one's own desires. Further, to use NFP effectively, the couple must come to greater trust in each other about their sexuality and to take all its aspects into account, thinking as a couple whose fertility is a property of the couple, not of either individual alone.

Dating

The same general principle applies to other sexual problems. For example, it helps to answer some of the questions that arise for youngsters when they begin to date and eventually seek to discover the person with whom they wish to spend the rest of their lives.

To gain some clarity in the difficult matter of necking and petting, recall that these actions, also, are symbolic. They signify in various ways the desire to give oneself to another and they manifest externally the feelings of the heart. Obviously, these actions lack the fullness of meaning found in intercourse. Many of them are far from being universal expressions of sexual love; the meaning of something like a kiss is largely a matter of convention, though there do seem to be natural gestures as well, such as fondling, embracing, and exposure.

But whether conventional or natural, what is most important about these activities is that they are all in some sense incomplete. They tend to arouse and stimulate but not to satisfy. Their thrill is quickly dulled by repetition. The couple then tends to go further, not because their love has grown that much—it often has not—but to find actions that renew the original sense of mutual affection, and also because these symbols are themselves exciting and tend to draw one toward still more stimulating action. Yet the unmarried are usually not able to say these things in truth to one another. For, caresses and embraces are the natural preludes to intercourse, intended by God as partial symbols only of love, by means of which the couple suitably prepare themselves physically, emotionally, and spiritually for consummation in intercourse.

If the couple is married, the place of these things is obvious. But if they are not married, there is a problem. They are not permitted to use these actions as a married couple does. They cannot say by these means that they belong to each other, that they want the other to be ready to receive the total gift of love. But just that is what these actions generally signify, which is why they are so stimulating even to those who, quite seriously, want no such stimulation. Clearly, too, a couple may not use these symbols of love primarily for their own gratification and pleasure—that would be a still greater lie, using these signs of self-giving simply in order to get for themselves. So it is evident that the unmarried may not embrace or caress each other for the sake of sexual arousal or pleasure. They may not consent to such stimulation, even if it should accidentally occur. To act otherwise would be a sort of fornication or masturbation in emotion and desire, even if not in act.

Well, then, let us suppose the common case of two people who like each other very much, who are genuinely interested in each other though not yet engaged, and who wish by their caresses to do nothing more than show something of their genuine affection for each other. They really respect each other and have drawn a line beyond which they never go. They see clearly enough how terrible a thing it would be to use these symbols of love as instruments to destroy the soul of a person they like—poor friendship, indeed!—or their own, and they want none of that. What then?

A problem still remains. If such actions are continued or repeated week after week, whether with the same person or with others, even though the couple never step across the line they have drawn, there is, in this constant use of a language intended to be only preliminary, in the repeated and unfulfilled use of these symbols of love, a wearing down of their meaning, a loss of sensitivity and expressiveness. When some day they wish to use these symbols to express the depths of the unique love to which they are then resolved to consecrate their whole lives, they find they don't know how. As with flags on the Fourth of July or at a political convention, as with the "Star-Spangled Banner" at ball games and graduations, it is hard to recapture the fullness of meaning.

For those not yet engaged, then, kissing, embracing, and caressing, at least if prolonged or intimate, seem out of place. The pleasure of emotional warmth and the expression of mutual sexual acceptability are not sufficient reasons under the circumstances to permit the degree of harm done to the couple's ability to manifest true love, even if there should be no danger of impurity.

Those who are engaged, since they are committed to each other, even though not yet fully, have sufficient reason to manifest their love, even by prolonged kissing and embracing. Their love has led them to an initial gift of themselves, even if still partial, and may be quite rightly shown by these natural symbols, provided, of course, that this leads neither of them into sin, provided they do not get themselves violently overwrought, and provided the engagement does not go on forever. For, once a couple foresees that their engagement has to be prolonged, then intimate kissing and embracing and other warm signs of affection should be accordingly widely spaced out and rare, precisely to avoid the dulling and growing stale of the signs of love.

THE RELIGIOUS SIGNIFICANCE OF MISUSE OF SEX

As Christians, however, what we have said is still insufficient. Thus far, we have restricted ourselves to the level of natural symbolism. But divine revelation has elevated this natural symbolism by putting it to use to tell us not merely about our own psyche but about God and His love for us. Thus the moral quality of various types of sexual activity should be clearer when we look at the things symbolized by these activities in the light of revelation. The Christian sees all sexual activity and judges of its rightness and wrongness by comparing what it signifies in itself with the truth he has from faith: his knowledge of the Father, who has regenerated us as His children in Christ, and his understanding of the union between Christ and His Church.

Christian Understanding of Sexual Lies

First consider the use of sexual activity to say what one does not truly mean in one's heart.

Speaking most generally, though we cannot see any necessity that God should have revealed Himself to us, yet, once He has done so, it is unthinkable that He should have lied to His people. Neither could God's Word lie to His bride. Of His very nature, He cannot, for His own purposes or pleasure, swear to her a permanence, a totality, an exclusivity of love which He does not have.

In particular, fornication, i.e., the sexual union of two unmarried people, symbolizes at the supernatural level the old paganisms. A man who fornicates could never represent the God who married Israel, who knew in advance her weaknesses and infidelities, yet who committed Himself to her alone forever. Nor could he represent Christ in His union with the Church, for whose purification from infidelity He willingly suffered torture and death. Rather, he would resemble one of the old pagan deities, who conferred their favors on their people as they themselves capriciously chose at the moment.

A woman who fornicates can only symbolize those ancient peoples who worshipped such deities. This worship was always conditioned. If their gods failed them in battle or in harvest, the people would either abandon them for the more powerful gods of their conquerors or add them as minor figures to an empirically more powerful pantheon. Of unconditional devotion, the pagans' religions knew nothing. Obviously, the fornicator could not represent the Church, to whom Christ has given His Holy Spirit to keep her faithful forever to Himself.

Adultery, on the other hand, denies the uniqueness of Christ or of His Church. A wife's adultery says in sign that there is some spouse suitable for the Church other than the Lord. Her adultery thus symbolizes the sin of idolatry when committed by believers, even as Israel before the Exile, while worshipping the LORD (Yahweh), still went after and worshipped foreign gods.

Conversely, a husband's adultery signifies in symbol that Christ could turn away at times from His only bride, the Church, and give Himself to some other, ignoring His marriage-covenant with her for whom He died.

If there has been in Judaism and in Christianity a sense that adultery by the wife is somehow even worse than adultery by the husband, one can see why. For, to deny the only true God and Jesus whom He sent is a greater sin than to deny the unique position of any creature, even the Church.

We can see also why adultery is not punishable by death under the New Law, though it was under the Old. For, Christ chose to take our sins upon Himself and to die for His sinful and adulterous people, so that His bride might be thenceforth without spot or wrinkle or any such thing. If, then, a wife's adultery is the graver sin, and yet the Husband suffered death in her stead, we cannot demand more than He; the servant is not greater than his Master.

Dissolution of a consummated, sacramental marriage is ruled out on the same grounds. Civil divorce there can be: separation from bed and board if a sufficiently grave crime has been committed by one spouse or the other. This would correspond to the Exile, to God's driving His people away into pagan lands, leaving them isolated and despised among those whose prosperity they had envied enough to worship their gods. Incapable of joining the pagans without total loss of identity, they yearned for the Lord but could not find Him until He had brought them to true repentance. But He could never simply abandon His people and, as seen in Chapter 5, could not, no matter what their iniquity, ever cast them finally aside to marry another; so also, Christian marriage cannot ever be dissolved.

This is an area where Catholics are, indeed, fortunate. For, despite the cultural decay produced by the social acceptance of state power to dissolve a marriage, they know that God has made the sacramental marriage-bond incapable of dissolution. It still remains possible for them to enter marriage in full love for one another, to give themselves without any restrictions, without any holding back. If their marriage fails tragically in human terms, the permanence of that bond is their strength. Unable to give up or surrender, they must labor and pray all the more vigorously to help each other to the perfection of love, even at the cost of great sacrifice. For they know, by the joining of their agony to Christ's, that sacrifice is the strongest language of love, beside which the act of intercourse itself is very little.

Similarly, insensitivity or frigidity, to the extent it is willed and chosen, is utterly alien to the Christian. How could Christ be indifferent or unconcerned with those who love Him, He who died for them? On the other hand, we children of the Church can, indeed, be cold to Christ, refuse Him support in His labors on behalf of all our race, pay Him no attention, not wish to hear Him speak. This is the sad state of tepidity, where Christians do little more than go through the external motions of their faith, content to be inert and uninterested in Christ. Yet the Spirit keeps the Church from such coolness to her Lord; and to act sexually so as to imply the contrary is evil.

Christian Understanding of Sexual Perversion

If we turn to the fraud, the counterfeit, the use of the sexual powers in other ways than God intends, we see, in general, that God cannot be thought to separate His love for us from His sharing His life with us by making us His sons in Christ. Neither could Christ delight Himself with His Church without granting her fruitfulness by the gift of His Spirit, nor could the Church receive and enjoy the gifts of the Holy Spirit, while refusing to be fruitful, refusing to give that life to others.

As to masturbation: Christ did not come to please Himself, as the Scriptures phrase it; He came to seek a bride. He did not stay by Himself. He came and sought out His people, at the risk of rejection—and indeed He was rejected. Yet, to His own great cost, He espoused her on the cross and made her fruitful by giving her His Spirit, that she might become the mother of all the living. Nor might the Church ever delight in the gifts of the Spirit in isolation, not seeking to share them with those who do not yet know Christ. Such a refusal of missionary endeavor could only bring decay and decline to the local church that so turned in upon itself.

To learn what male homosexual activity would symbolize in terms of Christ and the Church, we first must ask what masculine figure other than the Lord is shown us in revelation. Who besides the Lord takes the initiative? Who else is other than and radically different from the feminine creation? The Old Testament sets before us in this guise the lovers of Israel: foreign gods and the foreign states they rule. Many things are bound together here in the Bible—the gods, the nations who worshipped them, the technology which these nations had but Israel did not: chariots, horses, elephants, and weapons of war. These are all the things that were summed up, in Roman times when our Lord walked the earth, in the one word "Caesar."

Male homosexual activity, then, symbolizes at the supernatural level man as in love with one like himself, enamored of the strength of the state, seeking from it the strength to be savior of himself. It is a refusal of the femininity of the Church, her weakness in human terms. It signifies secular humanism, for which "the only God of man is man himself," refusing to accept the true otherness of God. The state, its technology, its power for war, its attempt to solve all problems independently of God or His Church, its taking all initiative to itself—this is indeed a male principle. But we know that Christ has not wedded Himself to the state, to technology, to secular "progress," or to war—however good these things may be in themselves when not loved but only rightly used. Christ is wedded only to His Church.

The only other masculine principle in Scripture is Satan, who sets himself up as God, who takes the initiative in tempting and deceiving the whole world, who apes God's majesty and His power to judge and condemn the sinner, but without understanding the love that God is. It is, then, no great surprise to find the frequent links in history between male homosexual activity and actual devil-worship.

As to lesbianism, the question must be asked in a similar fashion. What feminine figure or principle is given us in Scripture other than the Church? Who or what other also bears, brings forth, entices, responds to, and draws forth the male principle? The answer, clearly enough, is: God's good creation, the whole created order. Lesbianism, then, signifies a Church who would turn away from the Lord to embrace what is like herself: created, dependent for fruitfulness on union with Another who is *not* like herself, lovely with a beauty given by that Other, incapable of initiative with regard to God. What lesbianism symbolizes is not a Church at all but nature-worship, a worship of Isis or the Earth-Mother rather than Christ.

A seemingly similar feminine principle—though I know no scriptural warrant for saying so—is the psychologism of our present day. This is a fascination with the psychic interior of others, where the interest centers in the same sort of interior that the would-be knower has. He is not drawn by a true psychology or psychiatry, that is, by a desire to know another *in his otherness* in order to help him to help himself to psychic health. Rather, the "pop psychologist" seems to be looking for insight into what he senses to be askew within himself or trying to gain support and validation for himself in virtue of others' experiencing similar things. This essentially feminine-feminine relationship would again symbolize a Church turned away from God to the created world, but this time to the interior creation of the human heart.

Symbolically, contraceptive intercourse implies that God might give His grace and pour out His Holy Spirit without permitting them to have their fruit, without granting the Church to bear Him new children. Conversely, contraception signifies that God would not mind if His people were to enjoy the pleasures of His light and consolation and yet refuse to bear the fruits of grace: pure faith, strong hope, the vigorous activity of charity towards God and all His people, through lives of virtue after the example of our Lord.

Contraception has, however, another aspect. As a barrier to the effective power of one's love for one's partner, it symbolizes what happens when a person goes to Confession, drawn out of sentiment, say, for Christmas or

Easter, and deliberately withholds mention of some serious sin. This obstruction of the truth renders completely void the absolution received and adds to his prior sins the sin of sacrilege.

Contraception also resembles the act of those who go to Communion in a state of known mortal sin. Here also there is a withholding; a barrier is placed to the gift of all one's self. Although one is going through the motions of love and even though there may be a genuine urging and prompting by love, yet by the imposition of this barrier of attachment to sin or of shame to accept forgiveness, whatever love may be present is rendered fruitless and inefficacious. For in Communion God not only gives us all but asks all from us. So also, the contracepting partner withholds the procreative power of love, and thus knowingly refuses the total gift of himself. Barring the creaturely conditions for God's creating new life, even as the impenitent communicant bars the creaturely conditions for God's recreating the supernatural life, he symbolizes a violation of what is holy and commits something akin to sacrilege.

LIFE, DEATH, AND LOVE

One can summarize by pointing out that, at both the natural and the supernatural levels of symbolism, the perversions divert that which exists for the generation of new life into a refusal to let the generation of new life take place. At the least, this indicates a certain lack of hope, a discouragement as to the future. Instead of transmitting life to those who will live after us, whom we will see only beginning their lives, we find that the raising of children is too hard, too painful. We feel that it is too difficult to share life so intimately with another person where the other is so very different in body and heart—and, too often, also in mind—and so we back away into what is familiar and engage in some type of fraudulent relationship instead.

But more, there is a relation between sexual sin and

death that human beings have known for long generations. As we can see as far back as the epic poetry of Ugarit 4000 years ago, in the plays of Euripides 2400 years ago, in the gladiatorial shows of ancient Rome 1800 years ago, and in countless other cases, deviated sexual lust becomes blood-lust; frustration of the life-instincts begets the death-instinct. Separating the power to give life from those actions intended for the giving of life is a sort of killing, and ultimately symbolizes a putting to death.

The tragic linkage of male homosexual activity to suicide is well known. While exact numbers are hard to come by, the rate of suicide among the homosexually active seems to be twenty or more times higher than in the general population. While not as dramatic, something similar can be said of masturbation, though this seems more often a symbolic prelude, a sort of little suicide-in-advance, than its cause.

Academic ethicians usually see no relationship between contraception and abortion. They regard these two acts as wholly different from each other. One is merely a withholding of life; the other, the killing of an innocent person. Yet, as those in the pro-life movement have increasingly been discovering, a woman who repudiates contraceptively her partner's power over her body gradually slides psychologically to a point where she becomes willing to repudiate the fruit of that power if in fact it has begotten a child within her. A man most typically will resort to contraceptives out of subconscious self-hatred or fear of responsibility, not wanting to bring into the world another like himself or not daring to. It is all too easy for him, then, if a child has in fact been begotten, to choose, out of that same self-hatred or fear, not to allow this new one like himself and so frighteningly dependent on him to come to birth.

A bond between death and the misuse of sex is found not only in counterfeit sexuality but, somewhat differently, when natural intercourse is lyingly done. The lie is told because of a decision to follow one's desires regardless of cost. And, like a jinni from a magic lamp, what results from those brief moments of self-satisfying falsehood comes forth unforeseeably. Support from one's parents, spouse, or other relatives is often lacking or deficient under such circumstances; and selfishness, panicked and alone, can easily turn to savagery or to despair.

We know of David's adultery with Bathsheba, and his murder of her husband. Murderous jealousy easily brings men to kill women they think have betrayed them. Adolescent fornication has often led, in less permissive cultures than our own, to tragedy through the hopelessness of an adolescent sentimentality which has found no bounds, no limits, and which has not discovered the courage or the strength to intend what they are saying to one another by their sexual activity. In our culture, an undesired pregnancy is more commonly met by killing the child inside its mother through abortion than by the young parents' mutual murder or suicide pacts.

There is a deep connection between suffering and death, however, and genuine love. This is visible not merely negatively, in the sad consequences of the misuse of sex, but positively. True lovers have always sensed how much pain their choice steadfastly to love any human creature exposes them to. The Christian discovers the full depth of this connection in the cross of Christ. There we see what Love suffers for the sake of those who are loved. It is on the cross that Christ died for love of those who tormented Him, willing indeed to suffer, to be rejected, to be killed by the people He loved, since His death would bring their salvation. Anyone, then, who loves with the love of charity, that is, by the power of God's love, will suffer, and suffer deeply.

It is just this link between true love and suffering that is rejected by sexual sin. One refuses to risk the grief and pain that can be inflicted by a spouse or by children. One is drawn by desire or driven by passion. One insists on pleasure or, at least, a release of tension. In any case, one rejects the cross that is formed when sexual desire lies athwart the love of God, and refuses to suffer the pain of frustration.

The answer to all sexual problems, then, is to take up this cross, to return in repentance to Christ on his cross, to accept the suffering that charity will bring to our lives. There is no reason to despond or to yield if we are tempted to self-hatred because of our sexual sins, or to self-pity because of the harshness of the battle to be fought against them. In truth and in love we go to the Lord. He loves us. If we doubt it, let us look long in faith at the crucifix. There we will see what true love is. We will see that which united Christ with His Church. We will learn what it costs, indeed, to be husband or wife; but at the same time we will gain from Him the power and strength to pay what is needed.

There will be life-giving pleasure, too, according to our state of life, if we do not seek that pleasure at the expense of the cross. We will then also find rejoicing in our life and a foretaste of the delights of heaven, as we come to realize more deeply what it means that Christ died for love of us and to sense that we are beginning to love in some degree as He does.

7

Christ, Father of the World to Come: Virginity and Continence

We have looked at what sexual activity, as the language of true love, means by its very nature and also at the fullness of supernatural meaning given to it by Christ. We have also seen how the prescriptions of the Law as to sexual behavior have been given their fullest weight and meaning by the teaching of the New Testament.

It is true enough that much of what the Law prescribed or forbade in this area, since restricted by time, place, and culture, has not been taken over, at least literally, by the Church. But far from being abrogated as mere culturally conditioned and obsolete regulations, as some mistakenly hold today, those commands of the Law have been reasserted through the symbolic and, therefore, universal language of the New Testament in a purer and, from a merely natural viewpoint, much stricter form—just recall the Lord's words, "Everyone who looks at a woman lustfully has already committed adultery with her in his heart." Yet even this degree of virtue has been made possible for our weakness by the grace of Jesus' love. All the prescriptions of Christian sexual morality arise from the symbolism we have been considering and are dependent upon it. All of them, consequently, flow immediately and directly from what God has revealed about the nature of His love.

But an understanding of the supernatural glory of Christian marriage and sexual union and an understanding of why certain types of sexual activity are seriously wrong is not enough. God has told us much more about what our sexuality symbolizes and shows forth as we bear witness to Him in the world. Let us turn, then, to a very different sexual symbolism from the one we have just been looking at, that which the Scriptures employ to help us understand virginity and continence.

Symbolism of Premarital Chastity

The attitude of the Old Testament can be summed up quite briefly, in a few lines from the Song of Songs, where the spouse, who is God, speaks of His beloved Israel: "A garden enclosed is my sister, my bride; a garden enclosed, a fountain sealed" (4:12).

Physically the maidenhead is an enclosure, a bodily sealing off of a virgin. Symbolically, the world has always seen it as a sign of her reservation of herself, of her being sealed off against indiscriminate loves in order, ultimately, to be the sacred receptacle, the vessel within which God will bring about the mystery of a new life through the action of her husband. Consequently, throughout the Old Testament, although one finds no trace of a *state* of virginity, that is, of a mode of life in which a woman chose, for the love of God, to remain a virgin throughout her entire earthly existence, yet there is a great esteem for virginity, precisely as a preparation for marriage.

The virginity of a young man is not as obviously symbolic, because his body, unlike that of a woman, is the same after his first intercourse as before it. All the same, his virginity is heavily charged with symbolic meaning. For, to maintain his virginity, he must establish from early on a rational control over all the tremendous upbuilding drive and vigor of his sexual powers and appetites. Often enough, he will have to struggle vigorously. Erections, wet dreams, and other spontaneous sexual movements or desires may well be more frequent than were he finding a sexual outlet with a young woman or yielding to masturbation. Nonetheless, a young man is able, by the grace of Christ, to achieve and maintain an ever more mature control and mastery of his sexuality.

By establishing this control over that which is, so to speak, the pre-eminent element of opposition in the sub-rational world to the action of reason, he shows symbolically that he is capable and competent to subject the world to the good of his family-to-be, that he can provide for them by his labor in the world and can protect them from the forces of nature and from enemies. The symbolic meaning of a man's virginity, then, is a dominion over the subhuman world for the good of his prospective family that images God's dominion over the entire universe for the good of His family, the whole people of God.

Further, this mastery of his sexual desires symbolizes a man's freedom to procreate or not, as his truest love may move him. The importance of this freedom within marriage is obvious today in a culture which gives so great a value to regulation of family-size. But, for the Christian, whom God may call to a celibate life as priest or Religious as well as to marriage, this freedom is a basic aspect of the maturity he needs if he is to discern whither God is calling him. In this aspect, also, a man's virginity is a likeness in his very flesh to God, whose power to create, naturally or supernaturally, is infinitely free. Hence, too, a husband has in his family or in a familial context a headship that his wife does not.

This symbolism of premarital chastity also explains

something that is otherwise very difficult—especially for young people—to understand: how it is, in God's providence, that young men and women often have strong sexual desires, appetites, and emotions long years before they are morally free to use these powers and satisfy these appetites in marriage. It takes even longer for them to develop the intellectual and emotional maturity to enter marriage prudently. Yet they are physically capable and desirous of the act of intercourse; they are even physically capable of having children. Why should they be put under so much strain when they are not ripe for the satisfaction of those desires? What is the reason for this seeming dislocation in the course of nature?

The answer would seem to be this: A young person has to learn complete continence and to gain mastery of his sexual drives and desires before he is ready to give himself totally in marriage. Sexual intercourse is a symbol of loving self-gift of one spouse to the other. But a person who does not already possess himself, cannot give himself. If a husband is not capable of perfect self-control, he is incapable of giving himself perfectly to his wife. So, also, a wife must be mistress of her emotions and feelings if she is to yield herself in true freedom as a gift to her husband.

There is many a time, moreover, when husband and wife are obliged to self-control, continence, abstinence in the strictest sense—for example, if one's spouse is ill; immediately before and after childbirth; when they are separated from each other by business or war. Certainly their love can be no less then; yet love must show itself at these times precisely in total abstinence from sexual activity.

But there is still another aspect of premarital chastity that we ought not neglect. In practically all cultures—even in our own, although with our cultural deterioration it is no longer obvious among us—there are initiation rites that usher the boy at puberty into manhood. Only after these is he allowed to join the men in hunting or war or the other manly activities of the tribe or people. Only then is he one of the adults. In our country he enters into his majority, comes of age; he may vote, make contracts, dispose of property, and is subject to military service. Among Jews, he has his bar mitzvah, being made for the first time subject to the Law. In any case, some rite, ceremony, or symbolic gesture takes the boy into publicly recognized manhood with its duties and its privileges.

Given the nature of this transition, these rites are strongly related to the boy's sexual maturation, to his physical ability to beget a child. In those peoples where a girl also has a rite of passage, it is connected with her first menstruation, her ability to conceive.

The point of interest to us here is that these rituals are usually closely tied to the boy's ability to bear pain and to endure hardship in the context of hunting, fighting, and other modes of male activity. The rites are symbolic answers to the question: "Can he endure the suffering that naturally accompanies a man's contests with nature and with other men courageously enough to have sufficient chance to win out?" If a girl undergoes a rite of passage, it is generally more closely related to bearing the pains of childbirth or, occasionally, to other pains that a woman must endure among her people.

Consequently, some of these rites, especially in more primitive societies, have been exceedingly painful and bloody. Circumcision is one of the more common ones, practiced not on the infant, as among the Jews, but on the adolescent. There are many other rites of passage, both more painful and more dangerous.

All these rites seem to indicate that there is a need, deeply rooted in the human psyche, that this instinct which makes a man physically capable of procreation be somehow tied in with pain or suffering, with contest, and with victory, whether over other men in battle, or over animals killed in defense or hunted down for food.

The essential meaning of these rites can be seen when we look at Christian chastity. This is the Christian "rite of passage." There is no need for circumcision, for any other bloody and symbolic rite. Christian chastity is itself the symbol of both the suffering and the contest—the effort to control one's sexual drives is painful and difficult; dominance over them is the conquest and victory. Perfect chastity alone proves that a boy has become a man; that a girl has become a woman. Each person must be subjected to the inner conflict: to the deep, obscure, but powerful emotions of the girl; to the very obvious physical passion of the boy. Only by chastity can they give proof of themselves as men and women who are adults, who have matured enough to accept full responsibility for their sexual powers, not treating them as means for amusement or experimentation.

All too often, a boy tries to prove his manhood by imitating those whom he judges to be men, but who are not yet such, in one kind of sin against purity or another. He runs with the crowd. They are claiming to have intercourse with their girlfriends or with prostitutes. He thinks he must do the same to show himself a man. Or a girl seeks to prove her womanhood. She feels that she has been left out if she does not have intercourse; her companions are doing it; she cannot think herself a knowledgeable adult unless she has done so too. Yet fornication only proves that the young people are physically capable of engaging in intercourse and, cruelly, that they are not yet capable of acting as Christian adults.

The basic insight, then, found in the rites of passage of so many different cultures and expressed in so many barbarous ways, shows itself most perfectly and finds its fulfillment in Christian chastity. The boy, through manly effort and self-sacrifice, claims his manhood by control and mastery of his sexual passion, becoming a man like Christ, the sole example of perfect manhood. The girl moves into womanhood through her control of her emotions and her still merely instinctive desires for a love whose true nature she does not yet understand, subjecting these emotions and desires to the demands of a freely chosen love for Christ in chastity.

From all aspects of its symbolism, then, the total continence of unflawed virginity is not only the sole form of chastity for the unmarried but the most perfect possible preparation of both man and woman for marriage.

VIRGINITY AND FRUITFULNESS

A woman's virginity seems to have been universally recognized, even by the pagans, as relating her to God directly and not only as preparing her for His creating a child in her womb through the action of her husband. As far back as records of human religion go, we find that some women were consecrated as virgins in order to carry out religious functions, to be servants of the gods, or even to act as priestesses. The reason was simply that a virgin is sealed. Being closed off to man, she is symbolically consecrated to the divine.

So, also, through the whole course of Christian history, women have chosen to consecrate their virginity to Christ. They seek, as virgins sealed to all power but His Holy Spirit and as images of His bride the Church, to give Him in her name that exclusive love that is symbolized by marriage. Those we designate as nuns today were solemnly consecrated in early times under the hands of the bishop, showing the importance to the Church of those who manifest directly her pure love for her Lord. For, the Church is the unique bride of Christ; as St. Paul says to the Corinthians, she is a chaste virgin espoused to the one Lord (II *Cor.* 11:2). Spoken both to individuals and to the whole church in Corinth, this remark applies to the Church Universal and to each of us within it.

A man, too, can be directly related to God through perpetual virginity. A man's consecration to God, however, is not one of union so much as of oneness, of likeness, of identification, especially in action. Recall the passage in *Genesis* where the man names the animals before he receives the woman. Many commentators on Scripture take this as a statement, in ancient Near-Eastern symbolism, of man's power over creation; and they find in this the most obvious explanation of the phrase that man was made in the image and according to the likeness of God, i.e., man shares God's rule over the world. By his virginal dominion over his own sexual appetites, then, he gains a further way to image God, symbolically, with respect to His governance of the material world. For, it is a man's task to subdue the world not only for the good of his family but, ultimately, to make it subserve the glory of God by grace. A man labors that the whole temporal order be formed into an instrument for God's service and praise; he must, then, refuse to be enslaved to it as he finds it in his own flesh.

It has, of course, been seen by Christians from very early days that man's creation according to the image and likeness of God is also manifested through his spiritual powers of intellect and free will, which reflect the perfect spirituality of God. The virginal man's freedom with regard to marriage we have mentioned above, and the likeness to God he has thereby. But he has also a greater clarity or transparency of mind and heart for contemplation. The writings of the saints bear witness to this heightened contemplative power; the most persuasive witness, perhaps, is that of those married saints who came eventually to lives of total continence, such as St. Jane de Chantal, St. Thomas More, or St. Gregory of Nyssa.

A fairly clear parallelism exists between these relations to God and those we noted earlier as preparatory to raising a family. But the parallel can be carried further still, to spiritual fruitfulness and the raising of children for God directly. Thus, St. Joseph, a husband given wholly to his wife in love, remained always a virgin. He kept himself such initially, perhaps, because of his love for Mary, but permanently and principally in consecration to God. Yet Joseph is the man St. Luke refers to as the father of Jesus (*Lk.* 2:27,33,41,48). He is one who, without procreation, nonetheless took the place of human father to our Lord, and was more perfectly father to Him than any of us will ever be to our children according to the flesh.

This power of the consecrated virgin to be a parent, pre-eminently and spiritually, can be seen in greater detail in Mary, the mother of our Lord and, thus, of His body, the Church. Perfect virgin and perfect mother, she shows even more fully all aspects of the symbolism of virginity summed up entirely in one person. As a virgin, she was enclosed, reserved for God alone, having within her no rival love. And because she was perfectly reserved for God, without ever any flaw or withdrawal of her love, God chose her and came to her to work within her directly the same mystery of creation that He works indirectly in other women. But He came Himself, so that the Child formed of her was God, not merely man.

Thus, the virgin is one reserved for God alone, to whom He then comes in order, through the virgin, to give Himself to others. This explains something that has often bothered people about the sexual symbolism of the Scriptures: a seemingly strange union of the notions of virginity and fruitfulness. If one understands virginity properly, however, there is no contradiction. Christ is virginal, yet He is "Eternal Father" or "Father of the world to come" (*Is.* 9:6). St. Paul, while speaking of virginity, tells us that he wishes that all men were as he is, that is, virginal or at least perfect in celibate chastity; yet he says to his Corinthians: "Though you have countless guides in Christ, you do not have many fathers. For I have begotten you in Christ Jesus through the Gospel" (I *Cor.* 4:14-15).

This is the basis of the Religious life within the Church and is meant to be true, as well, of all who are celibate. They are to be fathers or mothers of great numbers of people, not just of one family begotten of their own flesh. Parents of all those whom Christ leads towards holiness through them, they find abundant fulfillment even in this life. Their joy is to nurture the divine life of those entrusted to them and to govern and discipline them for their more abundant growth.

Likewise, bishops, since called by their office to be totally devoted to their local church, have either not been married (whether in East or West) or, if married, have had to remain totally continent. Yet they are spoken of, after the example of St. Paul, not only as the shepherds but as the fathers of their people. The priests of the Latin Rite, celibate like the bishops because married in Christ to the Church, are also called "Father," as are monks in the East. So, also, in Religious Institutes, we speak of the founder of the Order or of the one who drew up the Institute—hence, of one who serves as model of that form of Religious life, living perfectly the life of celibate chastity—as "mother in Christ," or as "father in Christ." The fullness of virginity, then, requires the fruitfulness of a spiritual parenthood that has graver obligations than natural parents have.

EUNUCHS FOR THE KINGDOM

But what we have said is not yet quite the fullness of the symbolism of virginity in the Bible. Our Lord Himself uses still another sexual symbol when speaking of virginity, one that is strange enough to require some comment. Speaking of marriage, He described its original character and, on that basis, prohibited divorce-with-remarriage. The apostles took alarm at this, since the Law permitted divorce, and said to Him, "If such is the case of a man with his wife,"—i.e., if he is not able to divorce her—"it is not expedient to marry" (*Mt.* 19:3-10). A little cynical, perhaps, but their reaction. Our Lord replied: "Not all men can receive this precept, but only those to whom it is given. For there are eunuchs who have been so from their mother's womb, and there are eunuchs who have been made eunuchs by men, and there are eunuchs who have made themselves eunuchs for the sake of the kingdom of heaven. He who is able to receive this, let him receive it" (*Mt.* 19:11-12).

This is a cryptic statement. But "those to whom it is given" have always understood it. He is inviting men to a state of perfect celibacy, asking men—those who can receive it, as He put it—to live celibate lives. Those who can truly understand it are called never to marry.

But, and here is the strange thing, He uses as symbol of this a eunuch, a man who has been castrated, a man who, in consequence, is impotent and has no capacity for sexual intercourse. Christ says that there are some who are born this way and there are some who are made so by men—this refers to the eunuchs of the Oriental harems, an institution that was ancient even in His time—and then He says that those who remain celibate for the sake of the Kingdom of God are like these. Now, of course, one can say that what He means by this is that, just as the true physical eunuch is incapable of sexual intercourse, so those who are to be celibate for the Kingdom of God should be just as completely removed as the eunuch from all sexual activity, not through castration but through the fervor of their chastity.

True enough; but such exegesis does not exhaust the symbol which Christ is using here. Castration is a brutal and grave deprivation. Through it, a man loses much of what belongs to him as a man, something so important to him that many would declare it essential to his psychic stability and healthy self-image. Yet this loss, apparently, is something we should see in virginity itself.

The meaning would seem to be that virginity and celibacy are always relative goods. They are undertaken only for the sake of something else; they are not complete in themselves. They always represent a true deprivation of some present good for the sake of something which is still to come. They manifest, in one way or another, a love directed toward God or towards man which has not yet achieved its fulfillment and which deprives us of any possibility of fulfillment in this life. We are searching for Someone whom we desire to love far more than ourselves, who is present, who sometimes lets us feel His presence but will not, in this life, let us see His face.

For this reason, St. Thomas Aquinas speaks of virginity as something that would have had but a trivial place in the Garden of Eden had Adam and Eve not fallen into sin. For had man not sinned, there would have been no need of special preparation for marriage. Man would have had the necessary control without effort. There would have been no need for waiting, for this expectation and readying oneself for something still to come—whether union with another human being in marriage or with our Lord in heaven, outside this world and its conditions altogether, which is the hope of consecrated celibates and virgins, those who have made themselves eunuchs for the kingdom of God.

Our redemption, as wrought for us by our Lord and as shown us in His own Person, though it has its initiation and its beginning right now, looks forward to the *eschaton*: to the last age, to the end of the world, to the final judgment, to the new heaven and the new earth. Thus, only in Christ, who came into a fallen world to suffer and die and, only then, to enter into glory for its re-creation, is it possible to live in a *state* of virginity or celibate chastity. It is the state of those who are consecrated directly to God, who are willing to be sacrificed with Christ upon the cross, but who also hope and expect His direct action to raise them to new life even now, the life of mystical union with Him, yet know that the fulfillment of His action will come only at the end of time, not in this life.

Thus, those who are Religious must indeed experience serious deprivation, a sense of loss, a sense of nonfulfillment in their human nature and being. But it is a loss, a nonfulfillment for the sake of a vastly greater fulfillment.

Therefore, if Religious fail to give themselves to charity, actively and vigorously according to the special nature of their vocation and call, or if they seek to live more or less as other people do, apart from their celibate consecration, or if they repine or hold resentment for the concrete ways in which they have been forced to share Christ's cross as a result of others' malice or ineptitude, then they can easily fall away, as many a recent example shows.

If there is not an intense and consuming love for Christ, looking forward to His coming and regarding Him

as above everything else desirable, if He is not one's motive
in serving the poor, in preaching the faith to those who
have not yet heard the great good news of Him, in helping
people to be just and charitable to one another, then indeed
the purpose and the preparatory value of one's celibacy or
virginity has been lost. Then, not only does the Religious
feel castrated; he feels nothing to compensate for the pain
of this loss. He gains no sense of charity and divine life
growing actively and vigorously within, no sense of
development and being led toward final fulfillment. Then
by necessity the things of this world will take over,
fulfillment is sought through earthly means, and he will
refuse to live longer in the state of a eunuch for the sake of
the Kingdom.

But it is not Religious only that are invited to make
themselves eunuchs for the sake of the Kingdom. A validly
married Catholic whose spouse has gone off with another,
a man of strongly homosexual orientation, a woman of
deep maternal affection whom no one chooses to marry,
and many another unwilling celibate are all invited by
Christ to accept this "castration" for His sake and for a
fulfillment beyond this world. His language shows that He
knows the pain of what He is proposing to them; His grace
will grant them success if they seek it from Him.

FURTHER REFLECTIONS

Always there are these two aspects to virginity or
chaste celibacy: on the one hand, it is a preparation and a
readying of oneself for sharing in God's creative activity,
whether by the generating and raising of children or by
making the world a suitable place for the human family or
by bringing to the Church those meant to be her spiritual
children and helping them grow in Christ. On the other
hand, it is not merely a waiting and a longing but a
deprivation and a suffering albeit for the sake of a greater
good to come. But in both aspects, its ultimate meaning is
perfect love, a consecration of oneself to Christ loved

above all else, a love centered on the Lord Himself directly and without intermediary as well as through all those He loves.

The same two aspects are visible even in natural human love. Sometimes we read in literature or learn in actual fact of a man who has fallen deeply in love with a woman but who must wait for years because he is off at the wars or because she has not returned his love while he labors to win her affection. But he waits and keeps himself chaste for her sake indefinitely, year after year, in order that he may win her and be worthy of her. How many more women, through a fidelity that seems part of a woman's nature, have done as much for a man they love!

We can see, too, that it is impossible for a philosopher working simply as a philosopher, i.e., in the light of reason alone, to understand why the Church has defined that the state of virginity, for those who are called to it, is better and happier than the married state. As a philosopher, the most he can see is what man is by his very nature. What the philosopher sees is, so to speak, man unfallen, since man's nature is the same after the fall as before. Faith tells us, however, that man has fallen and that this state of virginity, precisely because of man's sinfulness, is a state which, *if* God calls him to it and *if* he lives it in its fullness, will more effectively ready him for close union with God than will marriage.

It is evident, then, how much nonsense has been written about the harm done by continence and virginity. There is no harm in perfect love; and since virginity has meaning only as a preparation for perfect love, there is no question of harm coming from its existence, whether it be directed toward the perfect love of husband or wife in marriage or toward the perfect love of God which consecrated virgins seek throughout their entire existence here on earth.

Psychological harm does come as the natural result of frustrated stimulation to people whose "chastity" is mere refraining from sexual intercourse without being grounded in charity. Refraining from physical action, they give free rein to their thoughts and desires. Interiorly at least, they are not pure or chaste. On the other hand, harm can come to those who fear sex, who see sin in every stirring of desire or passion, who do not learn as adolescents to distinguish between arousal or orgasm that is freely chosen and that which comes unbidden and unwilled. As a result, they refuse or are unable to live at ease and in peace with the sexual body that God has given them.

It is, then, of considerable importance to see that the state of virginity or the quasi-state of premarital chastity is always intended by God to aid us to grow in love of Him and of our fellowmen.

8

Integrity: the Victory of the Risen Christ

THE NATURE OF INTEGRITY

Virginity and every kind of chastity whether before marriage, in marriage, or apart from marriage in some form of celibate life are to be seen primarily as anticipations and expressions of love. Such chastity is love preparing to give itself, love still in expectation of total fulfillment, whether through the mutual self-giving of human marriage or through that direct gift of one's self to Christ that is the spiritual analog to marriage. In either case, one is given to Him through His espousal to the Church, awaiting the wedding feast and final union with Him we all will have, please God, in heaven.

All too often chastity has been considered as simply the avoidance of unchastity, as a successful guarding against sexual sin. But obviously, avoidance has its limits: when one has come to commit no sins at all against chastity, growth would have to cease. But if chastity is not mere avoidance of evil but is rather a mode or aspect of love, then since love can grow indefinitely, so can chastity. Indeed, chastity is the splendor of love, the radiance that shines forth from charity in those who have made this love of God and man the absolutely primary thing in their life. Their love is then capable of directing their sexual desires in full accord with faith. As charity grows, its splendor too will grow. Neither has any limits save our own failures.

If chastity is the splendor and the glory of charity, then we should see it in connection with that which is the origin and source of charity in us, namely, Christ's resurrection. By His rising we were justified and given newness of life in Him. He arose physically, bodily, in glory, still human, still male—His resurrection was a victory of human nature over sin, death, the devil, and all that world which is opposed to God. His ascension was His triumph. Through His enthronement at the Father's right hand, Jesus is able to make all His chosen ones partakers of His victory. As risen and glorified Lord, He shares with us what He won by His suffering and death.

Christ's victory, then, is our victory because individually and personally we are united with Him by the action of His Spirit as members of His Body. He has made a perfect atonement; now that we are one with Him, we are meant to share in its fruits. By the power of His grace working in the weakness of our flesh, we too can triumph over the world and the devil.

These things the early Christians were very much aware of; but we tend to forget them, and are a little surprised when we read in Scripture about the tremendous joy of the first Christians at their release from sin. Christ's triumph was the source of their happiness and joy, even in suffering and in persecution. Underlying all else in the different parts of the New Testament is this joy at the great good news: Christ has set us free from sin. The same tone is present in Ignatius of Antioch and Clement of Rome and, a hundred years later still, in Irenaeus—the tremendous joy of those for whom Christ had totally broken the chains of sin.

But today, all too often, we feel ourselves oppressed, dragged down by our weakness, and enchained by sin. Concupiscence, desire, and the heat of our passions seem to have made slaves of us again. If we don't actually fall, at least we are constantly battling; and we find this battling sufficiently tormenting that it deadens our joy in Christ. If we are honest, we have to admit at times that we aren't really all that happy and glad about our Lord's victory. We don't spontaneously sing to Him, preach Him, talk to others easily and gladly about Him. We don't feel that we really do share in His victory. We look forward to sharing in it eventually, but not now.

One can give many reasons for this state of affairs: our need for desolation and temptation to purify us of our hidden pride; the necessity for aridity to strengthen our prayer and selflessness of service; our own careless forgetting of His victory. But there is another question to consider here: what are we looking for and how we are meant to go about finding it?

As seen in the last chapter, Adam before the fall was free of any need to fight to control his passions. It was not that he could not feel sexual desire, anger, fear, or sadness. He could; but he felt them only in a well-ordered and suitable manner, when it was appropriate and right to feel them, when his mind, enlightened by faith, made evident the circumstances that called for them. Eve shared this gift, traditionally called "integrity" by theologians.

Thus, though Adam and Eve could have had intercourse when still unfallen—and, according to St. Thomas Aquinas, with far greater pleasure and delight than any couple could have since the fall—yet, until they desired it by a free and deliberate choice under God's grace, there would have been no stirring of passion or desire moving them to such action beforetimes, running ahead of their own free choice.

This gift of integrity belonged to Adam and Eve

before the fall but not after. Afterwards, they were naked before each other and were ashamed. The mere sight of nakedness left them feeling no longer innocent. The new Adam and the new Eve, Christ our Lord and His Mother, were gifted with this same integrity. Remaining wholly free from sin, they always possessed this perfect freedom from concupiscence, from any disordered drives of the flesh.

Unfortunately, we often tend to think of integrity as rather like castration, as if people who were integral had no passions: no fear, no sexual desire, no anger. Or else we think of integrity as somewhat like a bolt of lightning from God, by which He would move in on the instant to stop any inappropriate stirrings. It is, in any event, something we think He has given to certain rare individuals but not to others, as if that were the end of it. Christ did not obtain it for *us*, apparently; we are all too painfully aware of our own battles with passion and of the unruly strength of our desires.

But integrity was, very probably, quite different from such notions. Rather than being a sort of passivity, a lack of nonrational stirrings, a change of nature, as if one had no sexuality at all, it seems to have been a gift from God of perfect attention to the meaning of any sexual action envisaged, in full awareness of one's situation and concrete circumstances, along with an immediate perception of how that meaning fit or failed to fit those circumstances and situation. Thus, one was able to choose whatever activity was appropriate at that time, sexual or otherwise, to express one's love for God and one's fellowmen.

Consider, for example, a man and a woman who are just beginning sexual intercourse, who are fully aroused, but who have not yet come to orgasm. If there comes a flash of light, a sudden whiff of smoke, and a cry of "Fire!," they go no further. Immediately both deflate and are quickly set free of each other; they can rush for the children and take to safety. The mind's power of attention, then, is sufficiently strong, even at the most natural level of our lives, to have complete control over passion at its hottest, wildest, and strongest if the focus of attention is sharp and clear enough.

If we are right, then, as to the meaning of integrity, it is something to which man, even in his fallen state, might again approximate by the power and the grace of Christ. If one is truly close to Christ, if one's union with Him in prayer has become habitual, then it is indeed possible to see the beauty of a woman or of a man with immediate, even subconscious, understanding of its relation to God, to appreciate fully the greatness of God's gift to this person, yet to be repelled at once by the evil involved in any suggestion of unchaste action or desire.

Perhaps an example will illustrate this. There is a rather amusing story, apocryphal I fear, told of a very holy bishop, a saint whose name I've forgotten, at an early Council of the Church held at Antioch. One morning this bishop was standing with a number of other bishops out in front of the church. As they talked, a famous and beautiful courtesan, a prostitute who enjoyed the favors of the imperial court, came sauntering by displaying her wares. All of the bishops modestly dropped their eyes until she passed by, except this one. He watched her as she came; he watched her as she passed by; and he watched her as she went down the street. The other bishops looked up, saw him still gazing after her and immediately reprimanded him for letting his flesh dominate his spirit. He paid no attention, still watching her. Finally, he turned back and with a very deep sigh commented: "How terrible a thing it is that a woman gifted by God with so great a share of His own beauty should use it for the destruction of the souls of men." He turned and left the other bishops, went down the street after her, and converted her. History or parable, this shows, I think, the sort of integrity which can be achieved even in man's fallen state.

To regain such integrity in our present life requires effort. It is not achieved overnight. Yet any priest who has been around a while knows well enough that there are young men and women who, from the very beginning of their adolescence have learned how to do this. They have had struggles, sometimes very difficult ones; and yet, as they have grown and matured, they have managed to remain chaste. Those who do not so manage, who fall into one or other sort of sexual sin, will have further struggles, for like so many of God's gifts, integrity will not be given save to the victor in battle, since the victory itself is His gift. Still, for all, there is but the one basic pattern of effort and growth, in cooperation with the grace of God won for us by Christ.

Integrity, then, is within our reach, even if not totally or permanently; for it is never our possession as it was Adam's. But Christ's grace is waiting and the effort is one worth making; the results can be achieved, some of them in fairly short order.

It often requires a painful struggle to reach the first level (the basic conquest of chastity of which we have spoken). It requires less to maintain chastity and to advance in it thereafter, except on those occasions when, for better knowledge of ourselves and for our humility, God permits violent temptation to attack us. But for the most part, once gained, chastity enables us to live in great peace. As it grows—for, being a form of love, it can always grow—it suffuses us with a tranquil attentiveness that is a reasonable approximation to the integrity that Adam had before the fall or, better said, to the integrity of Christ our Lord, in which it is a sharing.

This fullness of chastity, then, is something that *can* be had and that gives great joy when possessed. It is something that every one of us can demand of our Lord in virtue of His resurrection and ascension. It is something He has promised us, if we will only cooperate with the grace that He has won for us.

THE ROAD TO INTEGRITY

The Scripture has given us some indication of what this kind of effort requires. When the people of Israel came out of Egypt and were journeying towards the Promised Land, they had to wander through waterless deserts till God would hear their prayers and let refreshment flow from the flinty rock. They had to battle enemies, the wandering tribes of the desert, and, still worse, the peoples who were already established at the borders of the land they hoped for: Amalekites, Ammonites, Moabites. There were constant confusions and bewilderments as they found themselves in situations they did not understand. They learned day by day what God wished of them; yet they disobeyed, rebelled, and often yearned to go back to the familiar things of Egypt—and to slavery.

So it is with ourselves as we seek to become chaste, remain chaste, or gain a chaste integrity. The effort thrusts us quickly into a desert; battles soon follow. We find enemies we had not expected, within ourselves, in unforeseen situations, among our friends. There is a lot of confusion and bewilderment at the unfamiliar psychological terrain that opens unconsolingly in front of us. This is particularly true in these days when, within the Church, especially in the matter of sexuality, there is revolt and rebellion even among priests and bishops, like the revolts of Korah, Dathan and Abiram, and the others who rose up against Moses.

Nonetheless, there is no reason for discouragement. Those who are faithful now in their efforts, even despite their falls, will, like those who were faithful then, succeed. As the great crime then, which blocked them out from the land of promise for thirty-eight years, was refusal to believe that God would give them the territory He had promised them, so for us, the one obstacle that can turn our lives to misery is the refusal to believe that God will give us the victory of perfect chastity. But things are better for us than for them, for we have the grace of Christ; and even if we have despaired, He will take us back if we are willing to turn and come.

There is, however, an error that priests, Religious, or others who seek to help people in sexual matters need to guard against: the seemingly charitable thought that, since the road that one has followed oneself in gaining some degree of chastity has been extremely difficult, one should seek to avoid having any one else follow it. We would spare others the pain of traveling so rough a road, not by accompanying and encouraging them as they traverse it but by directing them along some different path.

The Scripture would indicate, however, that there is no possibility of avoiding an arduous journey to the land of promise, especially if one has already seriously mistrusted the Lord's promise. Given our fallen nature, we can be sure that no other road is better, and that most other roads will simply lead further into a wilderness where neither chastity nor integrity can ever be found but only arid desolation and fiery serpents.

To achieve the chastity and integrity we desire, what is most needed, is union in heart and in mind with our Lord. We too often simply forget His victory. We fail to stay close to Him in our thoughts, though we can only share in His victory by being one with Him. Such conscious union is gained, first of all, through prayer.

St. Joseph offers us a marvelous example—he who married the Virgin to protect her and to safeguard her virginity. There can be no doubt about his manliness; he was the man God chose from whom Jesus learned what it is to be a man. Yet to live worthily for so long in close union with Mary, with no smallest defect of unchaste desire, Joseph could not have had an integrity much less than hers and Jesus'. However strong it was when he and Mary were espoused, it was by continuous converse with her and, far more, with Jesus that it grew with the vigor needed.

Since prayer is our chief mode of conversation with Christ and His mother, our enjoyment of their words and presence, it is easy to understand how St. Joseph, the patron of chastity for men, should be at the same time the patron of prayer for all. Thus St. Teresa of Avila sends us to him as the person from whom we can best learn how to pray on the mysteries of Christ. Coming to live with Jesus and Mary as he did, chastity will quickly grow within us.

Spiritual reading is also a great help. It not only gives us much to pray over but is an important way to learn His mind and attitudes in a day when one reads and hears so many things—and not only in movies, TV, and the other media—that are diametrically opposed and hostile to what Christianity requires of us in sexual matters. Self-control, mortification, and some suitable bodily penance are also needed.

But all these things are powerless and empty, even deceptive, without charity. If chastity is truly the splendor of charity, then, if there is no charity, if there is nothing to radiate, if there is nothing present to be splendid, one cannot be chaste no matter what penance, no matter what prayer, no matter what reading, no matter what other activities one engages in.

Youngsters will sometimes go to Communion daily or at least once a week, because they have a problem with chastity. They masturbate, fall when they are with their girl-friends, or whatever; and they have heard that the Eucharist is the sacrament that gives chastity. This is true, but they have misunderstood it. What they are thinking of is something that will magically quiet their passions or remove the temptations or at least give them, without further ado, the strength regularly to overcome the temptations.

They have not understood that the Eucharist is principally the sacrament of charity. No one has shown them that, if the Eucharist makes us share still more in the actual life of Christ Himself and offers us a greater intensity of that love by which He died for the salvation of all, then their whole life must be re-oriented outwards towards other people. Such a youngster needs to be taught the connection between chastity and charity and how the Eucharist will give him greater grace to turn away from himself and outward toward others, so that he can live as the servant and the slave of all, even as Christ did, who came not to be served but to serve.

We must, then, receive the sacraments—penance and the sacrament of the Eucharist—as often as we reasonably can. For, they are the essential substance that feeds the life of Christ within us. But, it is not good to eat heavily and never exercise. Without giving ourselves seriously to the practice of fraternal charity, we will slowly grow flabby spiritually and eventually fall ill and die.

So, the goal, the purpose, the focus of our reception of the sacraments must always be to let our Lord join us to Himself in His life of perfect charity. Charity is not just any love for others, but the love that grows from faith and gains its strength from hope. By it, we love God above every creature, because we know by faith that He alone is worthy of all praise, love, worship, and service. Since we believe that God created all men because He loves them all and desires the salvation of each, therefore we also love them—for God's sake, not because of their own good qualities. Whether we like them or not, we know that Christ loves them. His love is sufficient for us; and loving them, we know His love more fully in return. It is this love that makes us truly chaste; for, as already seen, any failure in chastity is somehow a turning away from this love.

The secret lies in love, just as the secret of all genuine sexual relationships is love: giving oneself or preparing to give oneself to the person beloved by the integral symbol of love. It is a matter of leaving childhood, where a person is solely a recipient of his parents' love, and entering adulthood, where he is fit to be a parent—of his own children or God's—where he is capable of giving love even if he receives little or no love in return, giving his own love constantly and firmly, even as God gives. Since He gave His only-begotten Son to suffer and die for all men, so we must be willing to suffer and to die out of love: to suffer and die for spouses and children, our own or others'—all of this for the sake of that perfect union with God which is our marriage with the Lamb of God in heaven forever.

Scripture References

Two in one flesh: Genesis 2:20-25; I Corinthians 6:16-17

Israel, bride of the LORD: Hosea 2:4-5,15,9,16-18,21;
    Jeremiah 3:1-12; Ezekiel 16; 23;
    Isaiah 54:4-7; 62:4-5
    Song of Solomon—entire.

The Church, bride of Christ: John 3:29; Matthew 22:1-14;
    Ephesians 5:25-33; Apocalypse (Revelation) 19:6-9; 21:2,9

Individual Christians wed to Christ: Matthew 9:1-15; 25:1-13
    II Corinthians 11:2

Virginity: Song of Solomon 4:12; 3:6-11; Jeremiah 18:13;
    I Corinthians 7:1,7-8,32-34

Eunuch-symbol: Matthew 19:10-12

Readings from the Fathers

St. Methodius of Olympus, *The Symposium: A Treatise on Chastity*, trans. Herbert Musurillo, S.J., Westminster (MD): Newman Press (1958) in *Ancient Christian Writers*, vol. 27.

St. John Chrysostom, *Commentary on the Letter to the Ephesians*, Homily 20, in vol. 13 of *A Select Library of Nicene and Post-Nicene Fathers of the Christian Church*, ed. P. Schaff and H. Wace, pp. 143-152. Also, in the same volume, his *Commentary on the Letter to the Colossians*, Homily 10, pp. 303-304, and Homily 12, pp. 317-321.

St. Augustine, Treatise 8 on John in the same *A Select Library* . . ., vol. 7, comments at some length on pp. 58ff., 63, 66-67 and also, in the same volume, in Homily 2 on the Letter of John, pp. 469-470, 473 and in Homily 9, pp. 516-519. *The Literal Meaning of Genesis* v. II, bk. 9, trans. John H. Taylor, S.J., in *Ancient Christian Writers*, vol. 42.

For further reading in the Fathers, cf. in: Quasten, *Patrology*, Westminster (MD): Newman Press, in the most recent edition available. Look in the indices at the back of each volume under "Marriage" and "Church" for references in the text, where you will find listings of available translations as well as of the original texts. Note too that Quasten will sometimes mention only in passing passages of some length and importance for our purpose here.

Other Readings

Vatican II, *The Church in the Modern World (Gaudium et Spes)*, ##47-52.

Pope John Paul II, Wednesday talks on human sexuality, collected in: *The Original Unity of Man and Woman; Blessed Are the Pure of Heart;* and *Reflections on Humanae Vitae,* Boston: St. Paul Editions (1981, 1983, 1984).

Pope John Paul II, *The Christian Family (Familiaris Consortio).*

Gustave Martelet, S.J., "The Church's Holiness and Religious Life," *Review for Religious 24,* 882; *25,* 32 and 246.

Paul M. Quay, S.J., "Contraception and Conjugal Love," *Theological Studies 22,* 18 (1961). A revised and expanded version appeared as *Contraception and Marital Love,* Family Life Bureau, USCC, 1312 Massachusetts Ave., N.W., Washington, D.C., 20005. For an understanding of the method of moral theology used here, cf. "The Theological Position and Role of Ethics," *Listening: Journal of Religion and Culture 18,* 260-274 (1983). For a sketch of the doctrine of recapitulation that is central there, but not developed, cf. Paul M. Quay, S.J., "The Theology of Recapitulation: Understanding the Development of Individuals and Cultures," in *The Dynamic Character of Christian Culture,* ed. P. J. Cataldo, New York: Society for Christian Culture & University Press of America (1984), pp. 57-95.